The Jubi

M. A. C. Horn

Capital Transport

First published 2000

ISBN 185414 220 8

Published in association with the Jubilee Line, London Underground Ltd,
by Capital Transport Publishing, 38 Long Elmes, Harrow Weald, Middlesex

Printed by CS Graphics, Singapore

The front cover painting is by Peter Green, GRA

The maps are by Mike Harris

CONTENTS

Stations between Baker Street and Stanmore were originally served by the Metropolitan Railway. The street level building at West Hampstead dates from 1898. Capital Transport

Metropolitan Railway days

The Jubilee Line runs between Stanmore, in London's leafy outer north-west suburbs to Stratford, in busy inner east London, by a route which is as varied as it is indirect. Wembley Park for sport and entertainment; St John's Wood for Cricket at Lords; Bond Street for London's (they say) most exclusive shops; Green Park for a summer stroll; Westminster – the seat of power; Waterloo, London's largest station and gateway to Europe, Southwark for the Cathedral and Shakespeare's Globe, London Bridge, probably the most famous bridge in the world, Bermondsey for the famous market; Canary Wharf for Europe's highest building (at the moment); North Greenwich for the Dome . . . Let it not be said the Jubilee Line fails to hit London's most interesting places, as well as some of its busiest transport corridors.

The Jubilee Line developed in phases, each with its own comparatively self-contained history. First, there is the early period when the Baker Street–Wembley section was built as part of the Metropolitan Railway's expansion into north west Middlesex in the latter part of the nineteenth century. It was this expansion which generated the development of new built-up areas across the Middlesex farmland.

The second phase of development arose from the need to relieve the chronically overcrowded inner suburban section of the Metropolitan Line, resulting in the local services being handed over initially to a new branch of the Bakerloo Line, and then to a new independent central London route which became known as the Jubilee Line. Thirdly, there is a phase relating to the extension of the Jubilee Line eastwards. A range of destinations having been considered, the line eventually took off towards Docklands, to stimulate the regeneration of the former docks area.

What is now the Jubilee Line emerged from inauspicious beginnings. London's first Underground line – the Metropolitan Railway – had opened for business in December 1863, operating steam-hauled trains between one terminus at Paddington and another at what is now Farringdon. The railway was soon extended to Moorgate Street, and subsequent extensions east and west were to produce what are now the Circle Line and Hammersmith and City Line, both run by the Metropolitan for the majority of their long lives. But the story of the Jubilee Line starts not so much with London's first underground line as with London's second, an allied company called the Metropolitan & St John's Wood Railway (M&SJWR).

The M&SJWR was promoted as an independent company in 1863 and was to run from Baker Street to the Finchley Road area, a distance of 2¼ miles. Though legally independent there were financial and administrative links with the Metropolitan, who stood to gain feeder traffic; indeed, the Metropolitan was to manage the operation. Although parliamentary authorisation was forthcoming in July 1864 there were to be serious difficulties in the raising of the money, a recurring theme for London railways. The upshot was that the scope of works was greatly simplified, and the line was constructed as a single track railway from Baker Street to Swiss Cottage only.

Whilst the line was single track (and almost all in tunnel) the stations at St Johns Wood Road, Marlborough Road, and Swiss Cottage were all equipped with double tracks in cutting, side platforms being provided; station buildings were single-storey brick structures. The signalling allowed the line to be run in three sections, but from around 1874 pilot working was adopted and the line was worked in two sections, the passing loop, signal box and second platform at Marlborough Road temporarily falling out of use.

The railway opened on 13th April 1868 but the operation could never be described as particularly successful from a financial viewpoint. The main objective at Finchley Road (with its possible traffic interchanges) had not been reached, nor had a proposed branch to Hampstead. Although the line ran through the London built up area, it was not densely populated and parallel roads were good; the limited train services were thus not unduly strained. Through services between Baker Street (M&SJWR station) and Moorgate Street were abandoned in March 1869 having proved an operational inconvenience; this, too, was hardly calculated to stimulate further demand. However unpromising the beginnings, the M&SJWR was to have a profound influence on future events with the line proving a valuable springboard for further expansion into the developing countryside.

London's borders were shifting rapidly outwards from the Swiss Cottage area, and powers were obtained for a north-westerly extension of the M&SJWR to Kingsbury in 1873 (the station was located where Neasden stands today and was opened as Kingsbury & Neasden). Doubling of the existing tunnels north of Baker Street was also provided for, although not completed until as late as 1882. In 1874, only a year after the Kingsbury bill received the Royal Assent, additional powers were obtained to extend further north-west to Harrow and beyond.

Construction began in 1878 in tunnel between Swiss Cottage and the new Finchley Road station, then continuing in open air through new stations at West Hampstead, Kilburn, Willesden Green and Kingsbury & Neasden; there were no other intermediate stations short of Harrow. Stations all had side platforms with steps leading to single-storey station buildings – that at Finchley Road being a little larger than the others. Today's Neasden station, though somewhat altered, contains some of its original features though the other stations are all rebuilt. At Kilburn the line was on a substantial length of viaduct, but otherwise earthworks were relatively minor. Slow progress was made because of harsh weather, and arrangements for opening to West Hampstead on 30th June 1879 were makeshift – a shuttle train to Swiss Cottage, calling at a temporary wooden platform at Finchley Road. However, on 24th November 1879 the full double track railway was available between Swiss Cottage and Willesden Green, with stations open and largely complete.

Work began on the projection of the line beyond Willesden Green early in 1879, and was sufficiently completed for the extension to Harrow to open on 2nd August 1880. Apart from the one intermediate station at Kingsbury & Neasden on this very thinly populated section the only other significant feature was the provision of a carriage and locomotive works just to its north, an essential ingredient on a rapidly expanding railway when the existing tiny (and increasingly ill-located) facilities at Edgware Road were becoming inadequate. The new carriage works (which included a gasworks) opened in 1882 and since the whole affair was located in open countryside the railway thoughtfully built over a hundred terraced houses nearby for the staff; the new locomotive works opened in 1883.

The Metropolitan Railway (Met) took over the M&SJWR in January 1883, although this was something of a formality – the Met was already pursuing a regime of expansion as though it were a main line railway and was fully exploiting the potential of the

M&SJWR to this end. From Harrow, Rickmansworth was reached in 1887 and Aylesbury in 1892, whence it continued along acquired metals to the remote Verney Junction, over 50 miles from Baker Street.

Perceiving a need to find ways of generating new traffic, the Metropolitan Railway had in 1890 purchased a large area of land called Wembley Park, on the south side of the line between Kingsbury & Neasden and Harrow. It was proposed to develop part of the area for housing and part as a sports, leisure and exhibition centre crowned by a massive tower inspired by the success of Eiffel's tower in Paris, completed in 1889. Such a complex was hoped to generate much new traffic from London, hence the provision of a new twin platform station – called Wembley Park in the absence of anything better. Although the first 200 ft high stage of the tower was completed (only a fifth of the intended final height) money difficulties and lack of interest meant the abandonment of the scheme, though the much later emergence of Wembley stadium on the very same site meant that some of the original aspirations were eventually to be met in grand manner.

During the 1880s and 1890s house-building proceeded rapidly between Kilburn and Willesden and a little beyond; to some extent this was fuelled by the Metropolitan Railway's property activities on its own surplus land, much of which was bought for just this purpose. The scale of development created a need for a new station known as Dollis Hill, between Willesden Green and Kingsbury & Neasden, opened on 1st October 1909. This station was built with an island platform with a ticket hall beneath, and subways leading to Gladstone Park and Chapter Road (though the latter did not open until December).

Northbound train at Neasden in 1896. The Met's combination of long-distance non-stop trains and local all-stations trains on a single pair of tracks made serious capacity difficulties, not solved until 1914. London Borough of Brent

The arrival of the Great Central Railway in 1899 threatened to over-tax the Metropolitan's increasingly busy inner section – at one point it was proposed that the new railway shared Baker Street for its London terminus. In the event Marylebone was settled upon and the Metropolitan agreed to quadruple the line between Harrow and Finchley Road, where the Marylebone approach tunnels began (the widened pair of lines were later leased to the Great Central, effectively denying the Met any use of them). Construction of the line was to have an impact on the Metropolitan's existing facilities. At West Hampstead there was insufficient space for the new tracks and the Metropolitan 'down' platform had to be removed; the existing 'up' platform was thus converted into an island (the first on the Metropolitan) and the tracks re-arranged to suit. A pair of sidings was installed just north of the station at the same time.

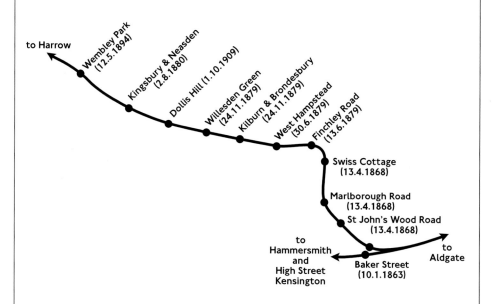

The Metropolitan Railway's extension into north-west London

to Harrow

Wembley Park (12.5.1894)

Kingsbury & Neasden (2.8.1880)

Dollis Hill (1.10.1909)

Willesden Green (24.11.1879)

Kilburn & Brondesbury (24.11.1879)

West Hampstead (30.6.1879)

Finchley Road (13.6.1879)

Swiss Cottage (13.4.1868)

Marlborough Road (13.4.1868)

St John's Wood Road (13.4.1868)

to Hammersmith and High Street Kensington

Baker Street (10.1.1863)

to Aldgate

Opened

Baker Street – Swiss Cottage	13.4.1868
Swiss Cottage – Finchley Road	13.6.1879
Finchley Road – West Hampstead	30.6.1879
West Hampstead – Willesden Green	24.11.1879
Willesden Green – Harrow-on-the-Hill	2.8.1880

Electrification of the Metropolitan's inner suburban services began on 1st January 1905 when the first electric multiple unit train entered regular passenger service on the Baker Street–Uxbridge all-stations route – by the end of March 1905 all the all-stations trains between Baker Street and Harrow were electric. Initially the trains comprised new saloon coaches intended for service on the Inner Circle (as the Circle Line was then called), but later the trains were worked by more suitable compartment stock coaches, though most were converted steam stock. The fast loco-hauled trains from Rickmansworth and beyond continued to be steam for a while, though some steam trains were reversed at Wembley where passengers were expected to continue to Baker Street by electric service. Matters improved when electric locomotives became available, and from 1st January 1907 all trains south of Wembley Park were electric, with steam and electric locomotives being switched there. The railway's power station was built at Neasden, to the north of Neasden works, and the power was supplied to substations at, among other places, Baker Street, Finchley Road, Neasden and Harrow.

With electrification came a desirable increase in train speeds and service volume. However, the improved services inevitably spurred new housing, especially in the London–Harrow corridor, and it was not long before the mixture of services seriously overtaxed the tracks south of Wembley Park. An attempt to improve matters south of Willesden Green resulted in the commissioning there of a bay road on 4th January 1906. This was on the north side, and was formed by conversion of the southbound platform into an island. A goods loop was installed beyond this for which the bay road also acted as an engine run-round. But this was hardly enough. Automatic signalling was to follow between Baker Street and Neasden during 1910/11, and this allowed the closure of a number of signal boxes. Direct current track circuits were employed, with pneumatically controlled semaphore signals and trainstop devices.

By 1912, the suburban traffic was slowly improving, and it was in that year that proper provision was again made for regular trains to run through to the City, the double junction at Baker Street being restored to facilitate the new service (though a limited through service had resumed three years earlier). New stations had also opened north of Wembley Park, though many were fairly primitive at first. Of course, traffic immediately responded so, despite the new signalling, capacity on the single pair of Metropolitan tracks south of Wembley Park was now under some pressure and was rapidly approaching its operational limit. The solution was to provide an additional pair of tracks between Wembley Park and Finchley Road, to be built mainly on the north side and intended principally for the use of the outer suburban fast services which were prone to delay amongst the all-stations trains. Four-tracking had to stop at Finchley Road as it was judged too difficult to duplicate the tunnels farther south, but with improvements at Baker Street and Finchley Road, and with the automatic signalling, it was felt that the railway could just cope without this luxury – at least for a while.

Work began in February 1912, and on 30th November 1913 the new lines were opened between Finchley Road and a temporary junction just south of Kilburn. South of Finchley Road station the tunnel had been opened out and replaced by a new covered way, large enough to accommodate a double junction from which point the new 'fast' lines originated. At the station the old side platforms were swept away and replaced by one wide new island platform serving what were now the 'slow' lines. A new, and somewhat smaller, station building was constructed at the same time, with entrances in Canfield Gardens and Finchley Road, with land available for commercial letting. At West Hampstead the new lines passed to the north of the existing tracks, requiring the West End Lane bridge to be lengthened.

The next section to open was that between Willesden Green and Neasden from 5th January 1914. At both these stations platforms were considered necessary on the fast lines. At Willesden Green the old southbound platform had already been converted into an island, the other face of which had served as a bay road. The complication here was to shoe-horn the new southbound 'fast' platform face into the space between the goods loop (which became the southbound fast line) and the adjacent road (Station Parade), accounting for the slightly odd arrangement found today; all the goods yard connections at the north end of the station needed re-arranging too. A similar approach was followed at Neasden, though without the same space constraints. At Dollis Hill the new tracks skirted the existing station on the north side. A nearby site was used as a massive spoil dump – created in line and level with the Willesden Green goods yard, of which it was presumably viewed as a possible future extension. At Neasden the station received a concrete footbridge, an early example of the use of that material in that form. No significant alterations were made at street level at any of these stations at this time.

A week later the 4-tracking was continued to Wembley Park, which already had four platforms, though considerable track alterations were made. Because of the location of Neasden Works, the 4-tracking was undertaken on the south side between Neasden and Wembley, the new tracks becoming the local lines. The final section was between Willesden Green and a point south of Kilburn where the works were most extensive; in particular there were two impressive steel bridges, one at Iverson Road of 99ft span, and another across Kilburn High Road of 147ft span. The latter meant re-arranging the entrance to Kilburn station, which was built into the northern bridge abutment. The new lines, which came into use on 31st May 1915, had no separate platforms at Kilburn, and the existing arrangements at platform level were retained.

Shortly after the dark days of the First World War a proposal for a massive trade exhibition was seized upon. By 1920 a government guarantee was forthcoming to fund what had become regarded as an essential tool for a post-war industrial resurgence – it was to be the British Empire Exhibition. A substantial tranche of the Wembley Park Estate land was identified as suitable, including the hill on which the ill-conceived Wembley Tower works had been located; indeed this precise point was to be in the centre of a gigantic sports stadium, first used for the Football Association Cup Final on 28th April 1923.

To the Metropolitan the exhibition and stadium were to be a godsend, promising considerable future traffic potential. By way of response, a new island platform was constructed just south-east of the road bridge at Wembley Park, together with a dedicated ticket hall and bridge leading into the exhibition grounds. The special station was operationally well placed for the new fast lines, to handle non-stop trains to and from London. The existing station was also considerably modified, with enlargement of stairs and ticket hall. The British Empire Exhibition lasted for two seasons, during 1924 and 1925, and was subsequently dismantled. A stadium, however, remains, and continues to provide facilities for an eclectic selection of events, including pop concerts and the Cup Final for which good access to the Underground remains an essential ingredient.

Subsequent adjustments to the layout of Wembley Park required rebuilding the exhibition station as a single platform affair, still south of the bridge, but retaining its usefulness for the special football traffic until 1937 when it was demolished to make way for other improvements; a new platform was built within the existing station to compensate.

10

Willesden Green, rebuilt by C.W. Clark in 1925 was typical of a number of stations rebuilt during the period. Clothed in cream faience tiling, the building had plenty of room for commercial activities as well as passengers. The platform buildings were not altered, some rebuilding at this level having taken place eleven years earlier. LT Museum

With increasing traffic levels during the 1920s it became obvious that some of the existing inner suburban stations were inadequate. At street level the degenerating facilities at St Johns Wood Road were much improved from October 1925 when a rebuilt structure was completed. This had a more prominent frontage designed by the Metropolitan's architect C.W. Clark; it was finished in cream faience tiling characteristic of the period and had space for commercial letting. The remainder of the station was improved and tiled at the same time, and the suffix 'Road' dropped. Willesden Green was reconstructed during the same period and the commodious street level frontage completed in September 1925. Swiss Cottage also received treatment. Here a new frontage onto the Finchley Road was provided as part of a shopping arcade, and the remainder of the station modernised. The work was completed in September 1929, again in Clark's faience-tiled style. The arcade and station entrance was demolished in the early 1960s in connection with a road widening scheme.

Trains were also lengthened, where possible to eight coaches, but this required significant platform lengthening works at a number of stations – especially the tunnel ones. At Swiss Cottage and Marlborough Road such expense was viewed as unwarranted and extensions in the form of narrow wooden catwalks were all that was provided; St Johns Wood was a little easier as one end was in the open air. Most of these works were complete by 1932.

The Metropolitan had kept a weather eye on the developing area north of Wembley Park lying roughly mid-way between its own line to Harrow and the rival Underground Group's Edgware branch, which opened in 1924 (the Underground Group owned the tube lines and most of the buses). Towards the end of the 1920s housing development seemed inevitable; the Canons Park estate land was for sale, and everywhere in the neighbourhood house-builders were applying pressure for improved transport facilities to help unlock the fortunes to be made.

Although the Metropolitan was nervous about further overloading the tunnels south of Finchley Road with trains from yet another branch, especially when traffic was growing heavily anyway, it was even more nervous about the likelihood of any financial return from a branch which ran into as yet quite undeveloped country. However in 1929 a welcome government guarantee for the necessary capital was forthcoming for both the branch and other capacity-relieving measures; it was in this climate that the decision to press on to Stanmore was taken.

The necessary works for the Stanmore extension were authorised in the Metropolitan's 1930 Act, and started in November of that year. The line was to be just over four miles long from its junction with new 'slow' lines half a mile to the north of Wembley Park station (4-tracking had just been extended to Harrow). The new branch was to curve sharply north-west beyond the junction and proceed to the terminus at Stanmore, situated about half a mile from the village. Intermediate stations were to be provided at Kingsbury Green and Canons Park (Edgware), though at opening the former was actually named 'Kingsbury', which village was actually some way to the south (to help avoid confusion, Neasden & Kingsbury station – which had been Kingsbury & Neasden until 1910 – helpfully lost its suffix at around the same time). Provision was also made for a third station between Kingsbury and Canons Park, contrived to be called 'Queensbury' but not immediately proceeded with.

The line at Canons Park straddles an almost deserted Whitchurch Lane soon after the opening of the Stanmore branch in 1932. Dennis Edwards collection

Map showing Stanmore Extension, taken from contemporary brochure. The station site at Queensbury is shown a little further north than as subsequently built. The original requirement was for a station just over 2 miles from the junction (it was built at 2¼ miles), so the map's suggested location at the as yet incomplete meeting of Taunton Way and Camrose Avenue is likely to be an error.

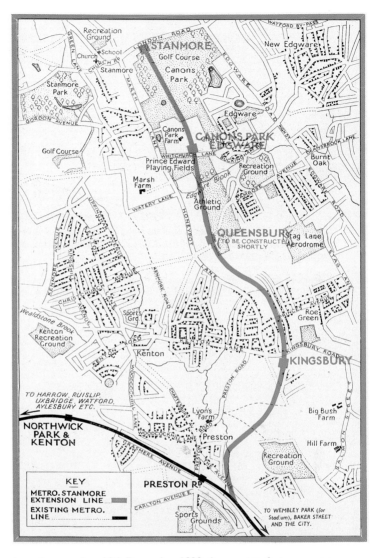

The Stanmore branch opened on 10th December 1932. Amongst its features was a form of signalling known as Centralised Traffic Control – the first installation outside the USA. This was a form of operation where instructions from, and indications to, the signal box at Wembley Park were transmitted over a dedicated 3-wire line in code. The electrical interlocking equipment at Stanmore was entirely unmanned. At Stanmore a 3-road goods yard was built to the east of the platforms; this was perhaps optimistically described by the Railway as 'spacious' – 'where coal and all classes of Building material can be expeditiously dealt with'. Two new substations were built, one at the junction for the branch near Preston Road and the other at Canons Park, with high tension power being supplied from Neasden.

13

Queensbury station, opened on 16th December 1934 and seen the following year. Three shop units remain to be let. The name is purely contrived as there was little else in the vicinity to suggest a name. LT Museum

Kingsbury station, shortly afer opening. Housing development is evident nearby, and the Metropolitan is seen heavily promoting its services along the undeveloped road frontage. LT Museum

The stations on the branch were in a similar style to those built a few years earlier on the Metropolitan's Watford extension, and were designed by C.W. Clark. Kingsbury and Stanmore had street level buildings in what has become known as the 'domestic' style. This used red brick, with a central ticket hall, canopied entrance flanked by shops and with flats above, located within a high pitched roof. At both stations steps led from the ticket halls down to platform level, with two side platforms at Kingsbury and an island at Stanmore. The arrangements at Canons Park were necessarily different as the railway was above road level; here a building astride the bridge was built, in a style more redolent of the 1930s. The ticket hall was beneath the tracks with canopied entrances immediately to the side of the bridge and with small buildings containing shops and first floor flats beyond; steps led up from the ticket hall to side platforms.

Queensbury station opened on 16th December 1934 when local building development warranted it (including much building construction across the former Stag Lane airfield, closed in 1932). To encourage matters the railway laid out some of the nearby streets, including Queensbury Circus, which is still owned by London Underground today. Although vaguely comparable in style with Stanmore, the Queensbury station edifice was very much larger, comprising ground floor shops and three levels of brick flats above, the top level built into the mansard roof in the usual style. The station entrance was a little lost in all this. The central booking-hall (equipped this time with a free-standing ticket booth) led to steps to the high level platforms behind the building.

One of the single-car trains (car 69) used on the Stanmore Line until traffic increased, shown just south of Stanmore.

The Metropolitan rightly claimed that the line would 'change the outlook and prospects of this interesting district', and that 'a healthy, vigorous residential development will take place'. 'One of the outstanding merits of the new line is speed. The journey time from Stanmore to Baker Street will be under half an hour, whilst the train service provided on the opening of the line will be particularly liberal and will total no fewer than 144 trains daily, which figure will be added to as traffic grows', said the brochure. 'The new extension will also prove a great convenience to those people wishing to attend the greyhound racing meetings, speedway meetings and other important sporting fixtures at the Wembley Stadium, for they will now be able to take the train from any of the stations on the new line direct to Wembley Park at which point a bus service connects with the stadium.' The Metropolitan's splendid salesmanship was rather misleading. The 144 trains meant trains in both directions, and of the 70 or so daily departures from Stanmore only 37 were through trains to Baker Street, and these were incomprehensibly timed; but this was a good service for the wooded fields and uninhabited building plots.

When London Transport took charge of the Metropolitan Railway in 1933 it inherited the brand new Stanmore branch, the development of which it felt minded to review. And thus it was just two years after opening that LT noted that the three shuttle and three 'through' trains per hour to Stanmore were 'in no way taxed' and that whilst building development had been slow, largely because of poor road access, there was nevertheless vigorous activity in the Kingsbury area. The design of stations caused some reflection and it was wondered if they had perhaps blended in a little too well with the surroundings, and remained undiscovered as the ready means of access to London. The fares levels were clearly causing some difficulty. The Metropolitan had been obliged to charge fares on the main line railway scale, with the result that the fare from (say) Stanmore to Moorgate was 1s 3d (6p), compared with 7d (3p) from nearby Edgware; equivalent monthly seasons were 34s (£1.70) from Stanmore and 24s 6d (£1.23) from Edgware. It was dryly observed that for this reason the sparse bus service feeders were actually drawing traffic away! Of course the Edgware line was known for its artificially low fares designed to encourage traffic development, but perversely that line was now overcrowded. It was recommended amongst other things that the Stanmore branch fares be brought down, better publicity be provided, including the new London Transport Bar & Circle signs prominently displayed, and that a car park be provided at Stanmore. The Bars & Circles arrived with commendable

Wembley Park signal box in early LT days. The panel on the right hand side contains the control equipment for Stanmore's short-lived Centralised Traffic Control apparatus.
LT Museum

speed, as did Stanmore's car park, opened on 6th May 1935; but fares harmonisation was not achieved until 1939, although 'cheap day returns' to the branch were introduced in 1936.

The Metropolitan had fully acknowledged the mounting problem arising on the 2-track section south of Finchley Road, and fully recognised that a thriving Stanmore branch, coupled with other rapid suburban development, would in due course bring matters towards crisis. The real pinch-point on this section was at Finchley Road station itself where four tracks converged into two by means of a flat junction just south of the station, with northbound fast trains and southbound slow trains fighting for priority.

Duplication of the old brick tunnels was regarded as impractical, which implied an entirely new route would need to be chosen. In 1925 the Metropolitan examined a scheme for building a tube line from Kilburn to Edgware Road station, running beneath that road itself, and promising some relief for the Finchley Road tunnels. The line was planned to leave the existing route north of Kilburn and drop down steeply into twin tube tunnels sufficiently large to accommodate the full-sized rolling stock. At the other end the line would rise to join the Inner Circle just west of Edgware Road (Metropolitan) station (though unhelpfully by means of a flat junction), and that station would be rebuilt. Intermediate stations were envisaged at Quex Road, Kilburn Park Road and Clifton Road. For several reasons nothing was done apart from the rebuilding of Edgware Road station itself, though with provision in the signalling for the new line when built.

In a desperate attempt to ease the congestion, Marlborough Road and St John's Wood stations were closed during the rush hours from 1929. While this helped the trains to a limited extent it did nothing for local passengers who were deprived of a station at the very time they most wanted to use it, and the practice gradually fell into decay.

In 1930 a further tube scheme was considered, this time running beneath the existing line to Baker Street, then rising to join the Inner Circle to the west of Great Portland Street station. This very expensive full-sized tube suggestion was also felt unjustified and a much simpler (but still costly) proposal was examined to replace the Finchley Road flat junction with a flying junction formed by a short tube line carrying the northbound fast trains beneath the slow lines just north of Swiss Cottage. This, too, was not proceeded with, and the Metropolitan's attention began to focus on the Company's wider short-term interests – its own independent survival.

By Bakerloo to Stanmore

On 1st July 1933 the components of today's London Underground, together with the buses and trams, came under the unified ownership of the new London Passenger Transport Board – more usually called London Transport. One of the features of the new Board was a remit to develop further and co-ordinate public transport facilities in London, an unenviable task given the phenomenal rate of growth of London at the time, and increasing difficulty in obtaining capital funding for much needed new works. At an early stage the Board formulated a co-ordinated grand scheme of new works with the main line railways, and were able to obtain a government guarantee for most of the £40m needed, to be raised through a shares issue (the value of which is about £2.5bn at today's prices). Thus was born the 1935-40 New Works Programme, of which the Metropolitan Line to Stanmore was to feature significantly.

The LPTB had soon come to terms with the difficulties of the Finchley Road–Baker Street tunnels, but the solution it adopted fulfilled not only the immediate objective of alleviating the bottleneck but in addition two wider objectives. Firstly it utilised some of the potential spare capacity of the Bakerloo Line south of Baker Street; the prevailing 24 trains per hour Bakerloo peak service could be increased to at least 32, it was considered, with fewer trains serving the Queen's Park–Paddington section which was slightly over-provided as things were. Secondly it supplied the Metropolitan Line with a much desired direct access to the West End from many inner-suburban stations, and a comparatively easy cross-platform interchange from all the others. The solution was to plug the Metropolitan relief tunnels into the Bakerloo; the proposal was included in the New Works scheme, but not in any detail.

Parliamentary powers were obtained in 1935 for a new line to run more or less beneath the existing Metropolitan Line, linking into the existing station at Swiss Cottage, which was to be retained. A new station was to be built in the St John's Wood area called Acacia Road, about mid-way between the existing St John's Wood and Marlborough Road stations both of which were to be closed (though it was initially thought desirable that the original St John's Wood would be opened for important cricket matches at Lords, which name it assumed from June 1939, five months before its closure). An earlier scheme for the route to run somewhat farther east, with Acacia Road station much nearer Primrose Hill, was evidently regarded as unsatisfactory, perhaps because it did not permit the closure of Marlborough Road and St John's Wood Road stations, which were operationally highly unsatisfactory. At Baker Street the new link met the Bakerloo just east of the existing station on the southbound line, and just to the west on the northbound line; this arrangement required an additional southbound platform and meant that trains converging at the junction could wait in platform areas.

It was intended that Bakerloo trains would be projected northwards over Metropolitan Line tracks and take over the majority of the local services. The northern terminus for the Bakerloo trains was left deliberately vague in 1935, and the plans would have allowed them to run both to Stanmore and Harrow-on-the-Hill. By late

St John's Wood as originally built. Flats have since been added above it. LT Museum

1936 train service details were being given tentative consideration and it was then evidently felt that the Bakerloo service should operate solely to the Stanmore branch, with part of the service reversing at Willesden Green and Wembley Park. The track layout at Wembley nevertheless continued to offer the opportunity to reach Harrow if desired subsequently, though this layout did nothing to improve the punctuality of the train services and was later altered.

Although the new arrangements were publicly promoted as an expansion of the Bakerloo Line, there is no doubt that the reality was at least as much the long-desired but now vital extension of the Metropolitan's 4-tracking southwards to Baker Street. The new and convenient interchange at Finchley Road meant that in practice the Metropolitan Line passengers gained the luxury of two central London routes.

Work began in April 1936 and was pushed ahead quickly. At Baker Street both the old and the new platforms straddled a new lower concourse area from which a pair of escalators rose up to meet an enlargement of the existing interchange concourse under the Metropolitan Line, to which it was linked by short stairways. A further pair of new escalators conveyed Bakerloo Line passengers to a new ticket hall area at street level, situated at the corner of upper Baker Street and Marylebone Road. This was connected to the existing Metropolitan Line ticket hall (next door but at a lower level) by stairs. The original Bakerloo ticket hall and lifts in upper Baker Street survived until after the Second World War, though they were little used.

At Acacia Road (which for a while was just called 'Acacia') and Swiss Cottage station sites new tube platforms were constructed astride a low-level concourse from which two escalators and a stairway linked the lower station with the ticket hall. At Acacia Road (renamed St John's Wood before opening) a drum-like ticket hall in brick was built at street level, the entrance flanked by a shop unit each side, all protected by an integral canopy; the drum stood proud of the other structures and incorporated a glazed aperture which illuminated the interior. After the war the ticket hall drum was incorporated into a new block of flats. To suit the new building line the station building was set back from the road intersection, a small garden intervening.

19

Swiss Cottage station at around the time of the Bakerloo's arrival in November 1939. The Metropolitan's station, which led off from the shopping arcade, survived until closure in 1940, but the entrance shown continued to serve the Bakerloo ticket hall by means of a subway. The building made way for road widening in the 1960s.
LT Museum

At Swiss Cottage the new ticket hall was below the road intersection and strategically located subways provided access to the world above and to the Metropolitan Line's ticket hall, arcade and platforms, which were to remain open. The twin tube tunnels rose steeply just north of Swiss Cottage and emerged at Finchley Road station which was completely rebuilt, though keeping much of the existing Clark facade. North of Finchley Road substantial changes were made to the existing infrastructure. The critical element was track re-arrangement so that the 'fast' lines would run astride the 'slow' lines, and not alongside them on the north-east side as constructed in 1914; thus re-arranged the centre (slow) tracks would serve all stations, and conflicting train movements were reduced to a minimum. This work not only required reversing the direction of running of the central pair of tracks but also necessitated major station alterations at Finchley Road, West Hampstead, Kilburn and Dollis Hill, where the existing platforms were in the wrong place for the new running

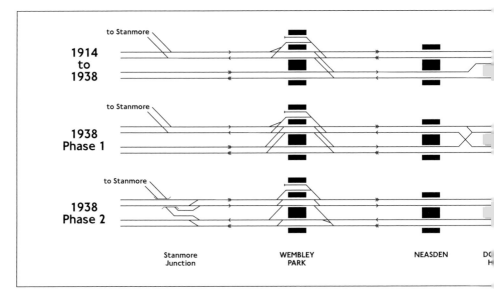

Subway to the old island platform at Dollis Hill & Gladstone Park, which needed to be resited in connection with the 1938 re-arrangement of tracks between Finchley Road and Wembley Park.
LT Museum

Below **Diagrams** showing the re-arrangement of tracks.

arrangements. An essential by-product of all this was comprehensive resignalling of all lines. At Finchley Road a second island platform was needed to service what were to be the new southbound tracks – the existing island was retained in a modified form for northbound services. At West Hampstead the island was in the wrong place and the only solution was to build a new one displaced sideways a few feet farther north-east, requiring some bridge alterations. Kilburn was fairly easy as the existing southbound platform could be adapted to form an island, with the old northbound platform abandoned. Dollis Hill, like West Hampstead, required bodily movement of the platform. Very little work was required to the stations at Willesden Green, Neasden or Wembley Park, where platforms already existed on all tracks. All stations between Finchley Road and Stanmore had platform heights adjusted to 'compromise' height to suit both Metropolitan Line and tube stock trains (except for platforms on the 'fast' lines).

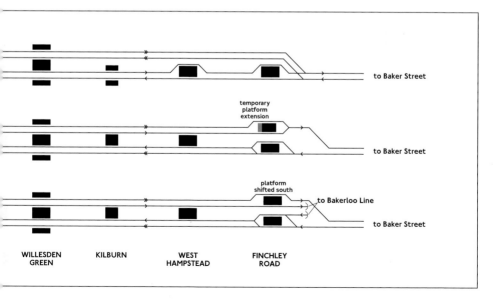

One of the earliest works to be completed was a new signal box at Finchley Road, commissioned on 25th July 1937. This was equipped with a 59-lever frame incorporating 'push-pull' route setting levers, and also controlled signalling at West Hampstead. Other new signal boxes (all with conventional single function levers) were brought into use at Stanmore (47 levers) on 29th May 1938, Neasden South (93 levers) on 27th June 1938, Willesden Green (59 levers) on 11th September 1938, and Neasden North (47 levers) on 22nd May 1939. The existing electrically interlocked cabin at Wembley Park was retained, although the signal frame was re-locked to suit the new layout. At Stanmore the signalling and pointwork were all-electric as it was not felt worthwhile to provide an air main – and so ended the very short life of the innovative CTC system installed by the Met. All the existing electro-mechanical signal boxes were closed during this period, and the intermediate electro-pneumatic semaphores were all replaced by coloured light signals worked by a.c. track circuits.

The biggest operation took place over the weekend of Saturday/Sunday 17th/18th September 1938 when the tracks between Finchley Road and Dollis Hill were re-organised into the form in which they are today. In essence the direction of running of the two centre tracks was reversed and they became the two new 'slow' lines. The outer pair of tracks (formerly northbound slow and southbound fast lines) became the new 'fast' lines, but retained their direction of running. This re-arrangement had a significant impact on those stations which did not already have platforms serving all tracks. During that weekend the island platform at West Hampstead had to be moved sideways by about ten feet with new track installed and old track removed. At Kilburn the former southbound local platform had already been widened into an island to serve both the local lines; the former northbound platform (now on the northbound fast line) was taken out of use and subsequently demolished. At Dollis Hill the platforms had to be moved bodily to locate between the new local lines, as had been done at West Hampstead. All was ready for traffic on Monday morning, though creditably it had been possible to operate a limited service on the Sunday too, all the more remarkable when it is considered that all the signalling was replaced at the same time, with new two-aspect coloured light signals, and with new track, points and sidings brought into use.

At Finchley Road the new island platform was commissioned between what were now to be the southbound tracks. South of the station the southbound line was diverted onto a new alignment for nearly a quarter of a mile, necessitated by the need to leave sufficient room for the future Bakerloo tunnels to surface. A temporary connection was made just south of the station to allow trains from what is now the southbound local line to join the new alignment; similarly on the northbound line a junction (this time permanent) just south of the station gave access to the new northbound local platform.

North of Dollis Hill the existing direction of running was unchanged, requiring a junction just north of the station where the two local lines crossed on the flat to resume their original direction of running. To control this critical junction a temporary 7-lever signalbox was provided at Dollis Hill. To reduce the pressure on this flat junction some southbound local trains from Wembley went along the fast lines until a point south of Neasden where a temporary crossover allowed them to resume the correct line before reaching Dollis Hill. From Monday 3rd October 1938 the revised direction of running was extended northwards to Northwick Park and the temporary crossover and signal box near Dollis Hill were removed. Track re-arrangement at Wembley Park included the replacement of the Stanmore Line junction with a new flyover. Again a limited service was maintained on the intervening Sunday.

At Finchley Road a second island platform was needed. This photo (taken from the 1914 island) shows the new platform under construction. Until the Bakerloo opened it was necessary for both faces of the new platform to connect to the Metropolitan's new southbound tunnel; only after could the platform be lengthened to its present position and the temporary entrance dispensed with. J. Bonell

Northbound Bakerloo (now Jubilee) Line tube (under construction) rising through the site of the former southbound Metropolitan single-bore tunnel just south of Finchley Road station. The photo is taken in the covered way built in 1912-14. To the left is the Bakerloo's southbound track where the covered way was extended. LT Museum

View along Christchurch Avenue, Brondesbury, showing Kilburn station on the right, built into the bridge abutment on the corner of Shoot Up Hill, and prior to the alterations in 1938/9 where a modernised frontage was provided. Although the station was formally Kilburn & Brondesbury until 1950, the suffix fell into rapid disuse in LT days as the new sign on the left shows. LT Museum

Most of the stations on this section were improved in some way. At West Hampstead the existing station building was retained but the interior was entirely refurbished to the latest standards. At platform level new station buildings were erected with integral canopy, and flower beds installed. At Kilburn the existing entrance and ticket hall were completely rebuilt and refurbished, although the former southbound stairs were retained in their original form; at platform level completely new structures were provided. Both Willesden Green and Neasden survived substantially unmolested. Dollis Hill received a modernised ticket hall, with necessary other adjustments to suit the resited platform above; again completely new platform facilities were provided. Wembley Park received some adjustments, but again remained largely unmodified.

One of the more pressing changes required by the arrival of the Bakerloo was the provision of proper maintenance facilities for the trains, the arrangements at the existing depots at London Road and Queen's Park were quite inadequate. The former Metropolitan Railway works was therefore replaced by a brand new maintenance depot which would provide the necessary facilities for both the Metropolitan and Bakerloo trains, the reconstruction being largely complete by 1939. At Stanmore (where the goods yard had closed in 1936, after only four years) six new running sidings were also laid.

West Hampstead station soon after the transfer to the Bakerloo Line. A northbound standard stock train is shown on the left and a southbound 1938 stock train on the right (the passenger door controls are visible but not being used). LT Museum

It was not until 2nd November 1939 that Bakerloo trains began operating between Stanmore and Elephant & Castle. Under the new arrangements services between Wembley Park and Stanmore were entirely handed over to Bakerloo Line trains, as were most of the local service between Wembley Park and Finchley Road. In the peaks six Metropolitan trains per hour called all-stations between Wembley Park and Baker Street, and certain other Metropolitan trains also called at Swiss Cottage; these did not continue beyond August 1940 when the Metropolitan ticket hall and platforms at Swiss Cottage were closed and all local trains between Wembley Park and Baker Street became Bakerloo. Initially, around just under half the Bakerloo service served the Stanmore branch, every 4 minutes in the peaks as far as Wembley Park, and 8 minutes to Stanmore. These gaps widened to 5 minutes and 10 minutes off-peaks, and 7½ minutes and 15 minutes on Sundays.

Trains were of six cars of 'standard' stock initially, although by 1942 the majority were of the new 1938 stock which had below-floor equipment and a somewhat higher passenger capacity (for which reason they were concentrated on the busier Queen's Park route). From 1946 platform extensions in central London allowed Bakerloo trains to be lengthened to seven cars, and there were only five old stock trains still running, which were very soon to be replaced.

In anticipation of a Bakerloo extension to Camberwell a new depot was planned at

Stanmore, though in the event just one new siding was added on 1st February 1952, just before the extension was formally cancelled because of lack of money. It was around 1948 that worries about the Stanmore services having overloaded the Bakerloo Line began to be ventilated, though that year was probably London Transport's busiest, with much of the system overloaded.

Pre-war normality resumed on the Bakerloo Line from June 1950 when short trains began to run during the slack periods; the 3-car portions of trains were stabled, leaving 4-car trains in service. This was the first time that short Bakerloo trains had run on the Stanmore branch. From December 1949 passenger door control was introduced on the open sections of the Bakerloo Line; this was a pre-war idea which had not been entirely satisfactory – the equipment was much modified as a result of the earlier experiences. The intention was that out of the rush hours passengers could open the doors next to them from nearby push buttons (under the overriding control of the guard); this cut down wear and tear on doors through which no-one wished to pass, and in cold weather helped to keep the cars warm. Neither passenger door control nor uncoupling proved sufficiently advantageous to outweigh the operational and maintenance complications which then resulted. They were abandoned respectively in 1959 and 1961.

It might also be mentioned here that Wembley Park station had been considerably expanded in preparation for the 1948 Olympic Games, focused on Wembley stadium. The old station building remained largely unaltered from Metropolitan Railway days, but to handle Olympic traffic a new station structure was built alongside connected by a wide gallery to stairways half-way along each platform. Although the Olympic ticket hall is not in use for every-day traffic, it remains an essential part of the station's ability to cater for the crowds travelling to the Wembley complex for major events.

1938 stock 4-car train at Dollis Hill in the early 1950s during the period when train lengths were reduced during off-peak times. LT Museum

It is perhaps of little surprise that the untidy track arrangements at Wembley Park were to prove an operational nightmare. Apart from the complicated platform working, the main problem was that what had by now grown to six tracks at Wembley Park station converged into four tracks for the half-mile to the junction where the Stanmore line peeled off. This meant Metropolitan Line 'slow' trains had to manoeuvre their way between either the Metropolitan 'fast' trains or the Bakerloo Line trains before regaining their own tracks. The answer was to construct an additional pair of tracks between Wembley Park and Stanmore Junction on the northern side, requiring demolition of part of a carriage shed; the opportunity was also taken to simplify considerably the track layout at Wembley Park station. The works were taken in hand in 1953 and the new southbound track commissioned on 27th June 1954, at which time a temporary 59-lever signal box was commissioned. The new northbound line was brought into use on 26th September 1954, segregating entirely the Metropolitan and Bakerloo services apart from a few empty stock movements. At the same time a push-button control desk was commissioned in the old signal box, operating by electro-pneumatic means part of the former signal frame which had been retained to provide the mechanical interlocking component (the electric locking being superseded).

In 1955 the signalling between Wembley Park Junction and Stanmore was modernised, with the 3-aspect Metropolitan signals replaced by LT's standard 2-aspect system. At the same time an air main was provided and trainstops and (at Stanmore) points were altered to standard electro-pneumatic operation.

View north from Wembley Park showing the track layout and train shed before the 1954 rearrangement.
LT Museum

A view after the rearrangement had been completed. The layout remains unchanged today, with the Jubilee Line and its centre siding just to the right of the 'T' sign.
LT Museum

Aspirations for a Fleet Line

During the late 1950s London Transport began detailed planning for a new cross-London tube line. It was intended to be the next major scheme after completion of the Victoria Line, whose construction was then believed imminent (the Victoria Line eventually opened between 1968 and 1971). This new line became known as the Fleet Line, in consequence of its proposed route beneath Fleet Street.

Although parliamentary powers were finally granted for the Fleet Line, its ultimate origin is perhaps obscure. It may fairly be described as a complex distillation of numerous earlier schemes, each of which was developed to achieve particular though discrete objectives. But it is probably not untrue to say that the Fleet Line was linked (however tenuously) with the plethora of schemes which were formulated both during and after the Second World War. As the Fleet Line scheme now takes the lead role in this emerging story of the Jubilee Line, it is therefore important to understand how its routeing evolved.

There is no single thread to this story, but several recurring themes arose both immediately before and after wartime: new areas of central London to be served, existing lines to be relieved, and in particular the problem of the inadequate services which were all that could be provided on the northern branches of the Bakerloo Line so long as they both converged on Baker Street – a problem identified worryingly quickly.

The 1939 Stanmore service had in some respects simply transferred the Metropolitan Line's problems to the tube services below. It was not possible to offer reliably much more than a 3½- to 4-minute interval service on either the Stanmore or Queen's Park branch, and traffic levels demanded better, particularly to Paddington. Similarly, the section of Bakerloo Line south of Baker Street was heavily overcrowded, and got worse post-war as bombed-out City businesses migrated to the West End. It was also feared problems would get even more acute once cross-platform interchange existed with the Victoria Line at Oxford Circus. Clearly urgent relief was required. Oddly, schemes for providing such relief were emerging on drawing boards even while the Baker Street–Finchley Road link was being constructed.

By the end of 1938, London Transport was anticipating rapid completion of the government assisted 1935-40 New Works Programme, and was turning its attention to another set of new works for which it anticipated further government help. With the benefit of hindsight this may now be judged to have been optimistic (notwithstanding the war), especially as the government were seeking to cut back the existing programme. And so it was that London Transport began devising a 1940-1950 New Works Programme. Much background work was done, and some schemes were comparatively well developed before the events of September 1939 put paid to them.

Sir Patrick Abercrombie's 1943 County of London Plan contained many aspirations for the post-war era, but was weak on the detail of London's transport requirements (although the detail behind the perhaps obsessive plans for the urgent removal of the cross-river railway bridges is a singular exception). Although somewhat tentative, the

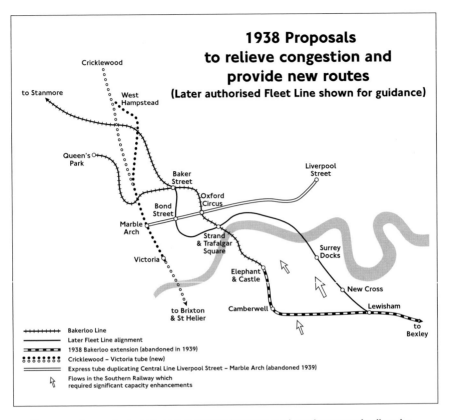

1938 Proposals to relieve congestion and provide new routes
(Later authorised Fleet Line shown for guidance)

Cricklewood

to Stanmore

West Hampstead

Queen's Park

Baker Street

Liverpool Street

Bond Street

Oxford Circus

Marble Arch

Strand & Trafalgar Square

Surrey Docks

Victoria

Elephant & Castle

New Cross

to Brixton & St Helier

Camberwell

Lewisham

to Bexley

+++++++ Bakerloo Line
———— Later Fleet Line alignment
▬▬▬▬ 1938 Bakerloo extension (abandoned in 1939)
oooooooo Cricklewood – Victoria tube (new)
═══════ Express tube duplicating Central Line Liverpool Street – Marble Arch (abandoned 1939)
↟ Flows in the Southern Railway which required significant capacity enhancements

Pre-war schemes included plans in 1938 to improve east-west communications by duplicating the Central Line between Liverpool Street and Marble Arch, and north-west to central London links with a new Cricklewood–Victoria line (with possible extension to the Mitcham area). A refinement of 1939 was to consider linking the (main line size) Cricklewood tube to the LNER Marylebone–Wycombe line near Kilburn, and to the LMS at Cricklewood itself. A Bakerloo extension beyond the already-authorised section to Camberwell in the direction of Lewisham was another 1938 scheme; this was intended to relieve the hard-pressed Southern Railway in the south-east suburbs which was also to obtain benefits from, for example, longer trains and platforms. Both the Lewisham extension and Central Line duplication had been dropped for technical or cost reasons in 1939, but had left a clear marker as to where congestion needed to be alleviated. In particular, a 1943 Ministry of War Transport study to consider post-war reconstruction, refers obliquely to these schemes and notes the overcrowding on the Baker Street to Oxford Circus section of the Bakerloo, already (after only four years) acknowledged to be a congestion problem.

limited railway proposals offer small clue to prevailing thinking. In essence the idea was to put the main line services using the Southern Railway's north-of-the-River stations underground and into a loop system, significantly focused along Fleet Street. The huge cost of £110–£180 meant there was little immediate chance of the aspirations coming to pass, and there was time for more considered thinking to take place.

With war out of the way a committee (the Railway [London Plan] Committee) was formed to give more detailed consideration to the railway requirements of a

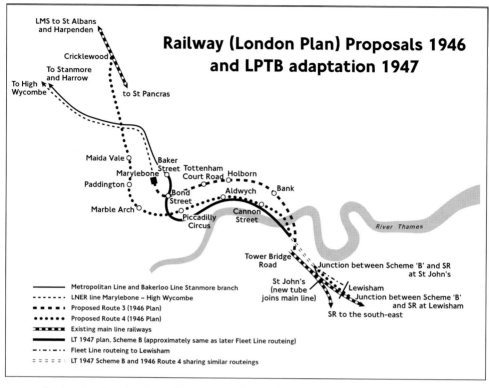

Railway (London Plan) Proposals 1946 and LPTB adaptation 1947

LMS to St Albans and Harpenden

Cricklewood

To Stanmore and Harrow

To High Wycombe

to St Pancras

Maida Vale

Marylebone

Baker Street

Paddington

Tottenham Court Road

Holborn

Bond Street

Aldwych

Bank

Marble Arch

Piccadilly Circus

Cannon Street

River Thames

Tower Bridge Road

Junction between Scheme 'B' and SR at St John's

St John's (new tube joins main line)

Lewisham

Junction between Scheme 'B' and SR at Lewisham

SR to the south-east

———————	Metropolitan Line and Bakerloo Line Stanmore branch
- - - - - - -	LNER line Marylebone – High Wycombe
■ ■ ■ ■ ■	Proposed Route 3 (1946 Plan)
● ● ● ● ●	Proposed Route 4 (1946 Plan)
▬▬▬▬▬	Existing main line railways
———————	LT 1947 plan, Scheme B (approximately same as later Fleet Line routeing)
— · — · — ·	Fleet Line routeing to Lewisham
= = = = =	LT 1947 Scheme B and 1946 Route 4 sharing similar routeings

The London Plan developed the pre-war schemes by linking relief in the north-west with that across the central London axis, along both Fleet Street and High Holborn. Route 4 was a development of the pre-war tube plan for a line between the LMS at Cricklewood and the Southern at Victoria, while Route 3 (along a slightly more north-easterly alignment) provided the link with the LNER near Marylebone. Both these tubes and others devised at the same time would be of 17ft diameter running tunnels with station tunnels some 650ft long with platforms 16ft wide. The proposal was to divert the majority of London Bridge trains to new through routes across London – an early form of CrossRail. Route 3 and some other new lines would join the Southern Railway near a new station at Tower Bridge Road, while Route 4 would join the Southern at Lewisham. In the LPTB 1947 plan (Scheme B) Routes 3 and 4 of the Railway (London Plan) Committee emerge in a revised, simplified, form.

reconstructed London based on Abercrombie's plan, and its final report was issued in 1946. Despite some practical reservations many of the proposals were inevitably focused on the perceived need to replace the river bridges with main line size tube tunnels, and the schemes sought to capitalise on this by continuing the tunnels north of the river to make useful cross-London connections with the northern main line railways. Abercrombie's tentative schemes were tactfully abandoned, and the committee clearly spelt out that loop working and inter-running of Underground and main line trains were to be avoided wherever possible.

Not very much was done to give effect to these proposals, whose immediate construction was out of the question for all sorts of reasons, particularly cost (equivalent prices today would be about £600m) but it did help shape later thinking.

In March 1947 an internal London Transport plan was circulated which approached the issues from a more railway-related angle and included operation over main line routes. The plan claimed to be based on the same principles as the London Plan Committee had proposed 'but with a variation in emphasis', words used perhaps to disguise downright disagreement. The basic north-west London, Mayfair, Fleet Street to south-east London theme of Route 4 was retained, but with relief given to Metropolitan Line services to Watford and Uxbridge rather than main line trains.

From 1st January 1948 both the London Passenger Transport Board and the main line railways were nationalised, and the assets vested in a new body called the British Transport Commission (BTC). Day-to-day control was delegated, respectively, to the London Transport and Railway Executives. The Commission had already realised that plans for London's railways should be re-evaluated in the light of its wider responsibilities and priorities. It formed a working party to look into these, which eventually reported in 1949 (the London Plan Working Party). In the meantime the new LTE began worrying itself with the issues and another internal plan emerged at the end of 1948 which took an even more radical (and expensive) approach.

The most relevant of the various proposals involved local services from Harrow-on-the-Hill and Stanmore (LT) which would be diverted at St John's Wood into a new tube to Marylebone, thence via Baker Street, Bond Street, Green Park, Westminster and back onto the existing Bakerloo at Lambeth North; this of course took advantage of the compromise height platforms which had been provided to Harrow. Beyond Elephant & Castle trains would be projected through new tube towards Denmark Hill, East Dulwich, Honor Oak and Forest Hill and thence onto the Southern Railway system.

This plan may have been useful in fuelling the debate about what should or should not be done next, but was hopelessly aspirational as it stood.

At a more strategic level the BTC published its London Plan Working Party report on 1st February 1949 and had alternative views on the future of the 1946 Routes 3 and 4, which were represented as its new 'Route F'. Of course, the innumerable lines drawn on maps represented only planning aspirations, and took little account of possible engineering or other practical difficulties which would have been encountered and might have had a bearing on routes as well as possibly pushing up costs. The ambitious proposals which concerned the planners during these five years make depressing reading in the light of the appalling post-war shortages of money and materials, especially steel. Not only did virtually nothing useful emerge from this period, but London Transport entered into a lengthy and sustained period of investment shortage, not seriously addressed until the 1970s and continuing to have an impact today. Apart from a large fleet of replacement trains in the period 1960-63 (which was essential), and the Victoria Line in 1967-71, very little of substance could be afforded.

So what happened to these plans? The annual report of 1949, the year following LT's busiest year thus far, refers to the need to 'clarify matters' (taking account of the population shift to the new towns) and the need to suggest a list of priorities. The 1950 report states that 'examination of some of the first priority works proposed in the report led to the conclusion that certain minor modifications in the original proposals would be desirable'; and that 'progress still depended on certain government decisions' (eg the future of the railway bridges). It did not bode well that the Bakerloo's modest Camberwell extension had been axed. The 1951 report revealed that consideration was still being given to the long-term proposals and that priorities were being reviewed in the light of present conditions. The 1952 report was silent and the final reference was in 1953 when it was indicated that in essence all efforts were now being directed

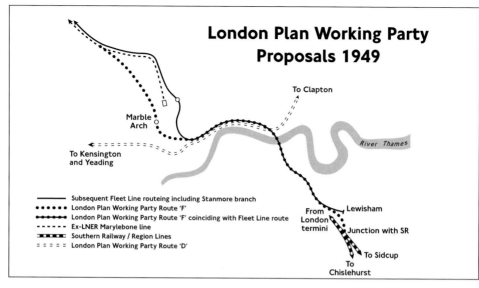

London Plan Working Party Proposals 1949

To Clapton

Marble
Arch

To Kensington
and Yeading

River Thames

——— Subsequent Fleet Line routeing including Stanmore branch
•••••• London Plan Working Party Route 'F'
•◆•◆•◆• London Plan Working Party Route 'F' coinciding with Fleet Line route
- - - - - Ex-LNER Marylebone line
▆▆▆▆▆ Southern Railway / Region Lines
= = = = = London Plan Working Party Route 'D'

From
London
termini

Lewisham

Junction with SR

To Sidcup

To
Chislehurst

One of the London Plan Working Party's schemes, Route F effectively superseded the 1946 Routes 3 and 4 and the even more similar 1947 Scheme B. It involved a new main line tube carrying SR trains from Kent via Fenchurch Street, Bank, Trafalgar Square, Marble Arch and Marylebone. From here trains would proceed up the old Great Central line splitting up at Neasden into the Wycombe and Aylesbury lines and via a new junction at Kenton where trains were also to proceed to Berkhamsted.

towards authorisation of 'Route C', the Victoria Line, and even that took another decade before money could be found. In fairness it should be said that traffic levels were now stabilising – 650m journeys in 1948 had risen to only 668m in 1962, on a somewhat larger system, so the pressure was to an extent less intense even if travelling conditions were uncomfortable.

The story resumes in 1963, from the beginning of which year London Transport and the main line railways again went their different ways and the BTC adventure scrapped. For several reasons this gave a slight boost to LT's resources as they were no longer shared (with perhaps diminishing priority) with the rapaciously hungry railway modernisation programme in which the emerging British Rail could loosely be described as being in the middle. But more significantly other circumstances had changed, in particular the climate in which expenditure on new public railway schemes was viewed. When financial authority for the Victoria Line had been given in 1962 it was not on the basis that it was likely to be a railway which repaid its financial cost. It had at last been recognised that the value of a well-planned, strategically placed new railway was to be reaped by London as a whole, and that it was not reasonable simply to look at the cash return to the operator. The developing science of cost/benefit analysis had reached the stage where the 'social benefits' could be realistically factored into the equations – or, rather, into 'railway' equations, for similar techniques had been used for new road construction for some time. Although this changed the outlook for future railway planning, it did not, of course, provide the money, and only the most persuasive cases were likely to untrap financial support from the public purse, whatever the benefits

Nevertheless it was natural that with the Victoria Line under way, thoughts should turn to the next major railway scheme. The majority of the 1940's proposals had by now truly died, having been largely overtaken by events. For example some of the pinch points had moved as a result of necessary but mundane capacity enhancements such as new trains and signalling and a slight slackening of demand. By now there had also been a slow dawn of reason (on the Thames bridges issue for example), and the omni-present shortage of funds meant that these highly ambitious and expensive plans could never be afforded in their present form.

But some problems had not gone away. The Stanmore line still meshed uncomfortably at Baker Street with the Paddington service, and serious overcrowding between Oxford Circus and Baker Street remained unaddressed, with fears of it getting much worse when the Victoria Line opened. The Mayfair area was still unserved and there was perceived to be an evident demand for a north-south tube. A tube feeder into the southern part of the (rapidly expanding) rebuilt City along the Fleet Street axis continued to be regarded as important, and there was still believed to be an opportunity (supported by the London County Council) to offer relief to the main line approaches to London from the south-east by means of a tube. A scheme roughly along the lines of the 1947 scheme 'B' thus began to emerge, but on a much simplified basis and planned as a traditional 12ft diameter tube, which somewhat circumscribed the opportunities for through-running, even from the LT lines in the north west, but it kept costs down and kept the scheme in the realm of the possible.

A joint working party (The Transport Planning Working Party for London) had been established between BR and LT on their formation as separate entities in 1963, with a remit to address transport planning issues in the London area jointly. An early reference to formative plans emerged early in 1964 when proposals for a Fleet Street tube were outlined. This would be linked to one or other of the Bakerloo branches north of Baker Street, thence run via Bond St, Green Park, Trafalgar Square/Strand, Aldwych, Ludgate Circus, Cannon Street, and Tower Hill/Fenchurch Street. The route beyond was less clearly defined with the line possibly picking up the East London Line to New Cross, and taking over a Southern Region (SR) line thereafter. The justification for the routeing was described as a need to provide relief to the Bakerloo and Central Lines, which risked over-crowding because of forecast population and employment changes, and also relief to inner suburban SR services.

In March 1965 LT and BR jointly presented 'A Railway Plan for London' as a preliminary report for internal circulation (a final – or public – report never appeared). In it was a definite proposal for construction of the new line, now given a name – the Fleet Line. The central London route was as just described, but plans had firmed up sufficiently to state that it was to be the Stanmore branch which would be absorbed, and that Cannon Street station could be 'double ended' and connected to Monument (perhaps replacing one or both District stations, which were very close together).

An alternative central London alignment was also being considered, running via St Paul's instead of Ludgate Circus, and designed to provide interchange with the Central Line and possibly Holborn Viaduct; however, engineering surveys and traffic studies for this alternative had not been undertaken at this stage.

The line would proceed to link to the East London Line and run to New Cross, from where trains would be projected over the SR either with the Bexleyheath line to Barnehurst, or the Mid-Kent line to Hayes, though it was not clear whether tracks would be shared. It was envisaged that the line would run in tube from a point north of New Cross to Lewisham Clock Tower, and that the East London service be confined to a Surrey Docks–Shoreditch (or Whitechapel) shuttle, with New Cross Gate abandoned. At this stage costs were estimated as likely to be in the order of £57m.

Beyond Lewisham the decision as to whether the Line should be linked to the Bexleyheath Line or the Mid-Kent Line to Hayes and Addiscombe was fairly evenly balanced. The argument was set out as follows:

Both lines extend a little beyond 12 miles from the centre of London, i.e. a little farther out than is desirable for an 'urban' type of service; but if an existing branch is to be absorbed into the Fleet Line, it must be one which can be severed from the Southern Region network without undue difficulty, and which allows scope for stabling and reversing facilities. The Mid-Kent Line is the more self contained. The Bexleyheath Line carries a heavier traffic volume to all the in-town areas which would be served by the Fleet Line, whilst traffic on the Mid-Kent Line is somewhat lighter. Residential areas near the Mid-Kent Line would continue to be served by the Southern Region giving a faster run to the London termini although, in terms of journeys to central London destinations which involve transfer to the central Underground system, a Mid-Kent Line tube service could still be competitive. In arriving at a decision on this point, an important factor would be the extent to which the Southern Region could close stations and withdraw services on other lines in the catchment area of the Mid-Kent Line, which would be in keeping with the streamlining of services on the approaches to British Railways termini to give faster long distance journeys. The transfer of either line would involve certain problems of accommodation for stabling trains.

The 1965 annual report revealed that planning was proceeding on the basis that parliamentary powers could be sought in the 1967/68 session, and construction started in 1969/70 with a view to completion in the mid-1970s. It was hoped that a detailed scheme could be completed by mid-1966 for discussion with the planning and other authorities concerned, which in the event it was. By mid-1966 an aerial survey was in progress, and borehole investigations were being made in the difficult ground on each side of the Thames and in the bed of the river itself. It was hoped that construction might start in 1969.

By the end of 1967 the first evidence became known of some nervousness about completion of the scheme in its full form, and by then the proposals had been also amended to throw grave doubts upon a service east of Lewisham (1965) and it had become necessary to retain New Cross Gate as a branch service (1966), abandonment having evidently proved unpalatable.

Detailed traffic estimates had by now been completed, one result of which being that both LT and BR concluded that consideration should be given to possible alternative eastern outlets for the line, instead of terminating it at Lewisham and New Cross Gate as previously planned. It was implied that this was a factor in deferring the seeking of powers until 1968, though just as likely was the government's stated need to restrict public expenditure which would in any case preclude a start on works until at least 1970. It was also stated, somewhat ominously, that: 'the first section of the new line to be built would be that between its junction with the existing Stanmore branch at Baker Street and a temporary terminus at Trafalgar Square/Strand; this limited section would give valuable relief to the Bakerloo Line north of Oxford Circus, which will come under increased traffic pressure when the Victoria Line is opened to Victoria in 1969'. The Public expenditure squeeze was perhaps to take advantage of the mounting indecision about the routeing of the line further east?

In the event parliamentary powers were obtained in the 1968/69 session, the Royal Assent being given on 25th July 1969, but only for Stage I of the line as far as Strand (though the powers actually permitted construction to a point 110 yards east of the junction of Strand and Montreal Place, a matter of feet from Aldwych station). In the meantime a 'firm line' for the route had been completed as far as Fenchurch Street, and it was intended to seek powers for that in the next session (unfortunately Parliament was dissolved in May 1970 and the Bill for the second stage had to be held over until the 1970/71 session). By early 1969 further studies had also been completed on alternative schemes for the alignment and terminals south-east of Fenchurch Street and their effects on the traffic and social benefit prospects of the whole project.

Parliamentary powers were just one hurdle: they didn't generate the funding. In September 1969 London Transport sought approval for the project and submitted the results of their detailed traffic, financial and social benefit studies for the Fleet Line to the Ministry of Transport. However, the proposal was only firm to the extent of the line reaching New Cross and New Cross Gate; LT wanted it projected at least as far as Lewisham, one of the six 'strategic centres' specified in the Greater London Development Plan, but was evidently not receiving very much support. By now costs had risen to £74 million (including rolling stock), but it was unclear as to whether this included the proposed Lewisham section.

Whilst Fleet Line plans were developing, a major new player entered the debate in the form of the Greater London Council (the GLC) formed in 1965. This body had significantly greater planning responsibilities than the old London County Council, whose authority in any case only covered what is now known as inner London. The GLC was keen to assume control of London Transport, which it in due course achieved on 1st January 1970, but not if LT were to be 'crippled' by having to meet the entire cost of the Fleet Line. Discussions thus took place between the GLC and the government with transfer of LT control in mind, although the touchy Fleet Line funding issue remained central. As a significant gesture the GLC offered to pay 25 per cent of the Fleet Line's costs, but the critical government support for the balance was to take somewhat longer.

To help discharge the statutory responsibility for co-operation between the agencies responsible for transport in London, a Greater London Transport Group was established early in 1970, under the chairmanship of the GLC. Following deliberation by the Department of Transport on the Fleet Line, the GLTG was also invited to examine the proposals. They concluded that there 'were strong arguments on planning grounds for building the line on its proposed alignment between Baker Street and Surrey Docks', and thought that 'it should terminate at Lewisham rather than New Cross.'

Using this as the green light, London Transport formally applied to the GLC in May 1970 for authority to construct the entire line to Lewisham, at a cost of roughly £86m. Although the Council approved this in July 1970, and agreed to meet 25 per cent of the costs, the approval was necessarily conditional on the government meeting the remaining 75 per cent. Formal application was accordingly made for this funding, but no response was immediately forthcoming. It was not until 18th August 1971 that the Secretary of State for the Environment was moved to respond, stating that he was prepared to provide a 75 per cent infrastructure grant but only towards the £35m costs of Stage 1 of the Line to Strand, including sufficient new trains to operate a Stanmore–Strand service.

The official justification for delaying a decision on the remainder of the line was government acknowledgement of the rapid decay of business in London's docks. It was now recognised that significant redevelopment of the area would in due course be necessary, and that it would have an impact on transport requirements. In consequence the Secretary of State had been minded in May 1971 to commission a report to investigate the Docklands redevelopment opportunities, so in August he was able to state that he would revisit the matter of the later Fleet Line stages when the report was available and the future development of the area was understood. A further and perhaps more pertinent justification for the delay in authorising the Line was limited funding. On the same day as the Secretary of State announced the Fleet Line go-ahead he also authorised the grant for the electrification of the Great Northern suburban services and refurbishment of the old Great Northern & City branch. By coupling the events he was able to say that by some way it was the biggest grant towards public transport ever given (and he said it in a way which clearly spelt out that the coffers were now empty).

The comparatively high price for Fleet Line Stage 1 disguises the built-in cost of providing a new maintenance depot for the Bakerloo Line. Transfer of the Stanmore branch to the Fleet Line would mean the Bakerloo would no longer have ready access to Neasden depot for routine maintenance, and it was impracticable to upgrade the Bakerloo's existing stabling points at Croxley Green, Queen's Park or London Road. A location near Stonebridge Park BR station was finally selected and constructed, but not without considerable difficulty and delay.

Meanwhile, delayed parliamentary authority for construction of Stage 2 of the Fleet Line was granted on 27th July 1971, with authority for Stage 3 sought in a second bill in that session and granted on 5th August 1971, but only as far as New Cross. The final 2257 yards from New Cross to Lewisham town centre required a further bill and was not given the Royal Assent until 9th August 1972.

The route south of Baker Street was to be deep level tube and envisaged twin platform stations to Fenchurch Street, with a scissors crossover west of Charing Cross and a trailing crossover and reversing siding east of Fenchurch Street, located between the running lines. The tube tunnels were to continue to Surrey Docks where the existing open air station would be used, with the East London Line terminating in a bay platform on the east side. The existing surface formation was to be used on the New Cross Gate branch, with trains terminating in the existing single platform on the east side of the station. Southbound trains for Lewisham would branch off at Canal Junction and follow the existing surface route to New Cross and thence into tunnel to Lewisham. Northbound trains from Lewisham would run in tunnel most of the way to Surrey Docks, meeting the New Cross Gate line by flying junction just south of the station; a tube level platform would be built at New Cross. A depot serving the Fleet and East London Lines was to be built just south of Surrey Docks on the west side of the line.

The disused bay at Surrey Docks which would have been brought into use for the terminating East London Line service had the Fleet Line extension through there been realised.

Almost perversely, a 200-yard section of Stage 3 was actually built. In 1972 LT exercised its Fleet Line powers to build an experimental section of running tunnel near New Cross in order to try out a new type of tunnelling shield; this used a 'Bentonite' slurry to improve ground conditions at the cutting face, which was advantageous outside the London clay belt which characterised south-east London. The work was undertaken in conjunction with the National Research & Development Corporation, and created interest around the world. Built along the alignment of the northbound Fleet Line, and beneath a disused link to the East London Line, it has never, and probably never will, see a train. As an engineering experiment, it was a success and yielded much useful information.

Tunnel working face at New Cross for the 'Bentonite' shield experimental tunnel. The back of the shield is visible with the hydraulic rams pushing against the completed tunnel to propel the shield forward. The two large hinged arms are segment erectors, ready to place new segments against the completed face when the jacks have retracted. LT Museum

The Jubilee Line

With the go-ahead given for Fleet Line Stage I in August 1971 preliminary works began within a few weeks, the first evidence being near Bond Street station where exploration began to establish what services lay beneath the road surface.

The main tunnelling began in February 1972 and proceeded rapidly. By the end of 1973 some three quarters of the running tunnels had been completed and three of the seven station tunnels had been bored, with two others and the Strand crossover under construction. The civil engineering elements of the station and running tunnels were completed by the end of 1974, including the 'step-plates' with the existing Bakerloo tunnels at Baker Street, where the new line would branch off. By the end of 1975 nearly all the civil engineering was complete and track laying well advanced.

The new railway had to be welded into the old at Baker Street. The southbound Fleet Line track was to branch left from the Bakerloo Line just south of the Stanmore branch platform at Baker Street, and proceed to Bond Street on a gentle right hand curve, crossing the Central Line almost perpendicularly. The northbound line was to meet the Stanmore branch somewhat to the north-east of Baker Street, and have its own new platform at the same level as the northbound Bakerloo, to which it would be linked by interconnecting passageways. This arrangement provided same level interchange between the Bakerloo and Fleet Lines in both directions of travel, minimising so far as possible the inconvenience of changing trains – although the constraints of station design made some of these passages quite long. In most other respects Baker Street station was not significantly further altered.

At Bond Street the existing ticket hall with its two escalators was barely adequate for the prevailing Central Line traffic let alone anything new; with the Fleet Line, usage was expected to rise from 12m to 20m a year. Here complete reconstruction was essential, and a spacious new ticket hall was planned, largely beneath the roadway.

Bond Street was a very awkward station dating from 1900. It served just the Central Line, whose platforms ran east-west immediately beneath Oxford Street. The original station building was on the south side of that road, with lifts connecting with a lower landing level from which two passageways led to the platforms. The ticket hall had been reconstructed at basement level in the 1920s, when a pair of escalators had substituted for lifts. But site conditions required the escalators to descend underneath Oxford Street to a lower landing on the north side of the road, with two, somewhat long, passages doubling back to reach the original access stairs between the platforms. These arrangements needed to be comprehensively upgraded to deal with the Fleet Line traffic, and a much enlarged ticket hall was envisaged spilling beneath Davies Street, Oxford Street and the lower levels of a new shopping development (called 'West One') to the west of Davies Street.

To facilitate the works a 600 ton elevated steel deck was erected over the junction of Oxford Street, Davies Street and Stratford Place. Installed in 1972 over the late-summer (August) bank holiday weekend, it facilitated construction of the enlarged ticket hall beneath, leaving the existing ticket hall area intact for the time being. Work

The new Jubilee Line required additional passages at Baker Street. This photo shows a new passage about to cross the southbound (Stanmore branch) platform around 1976, and awaiting installation of the bridge. LT Museum

did not simply include diversion of the usual gas, water, electricity and communications services – it included diversion of the Northern Outfall Sewer, one of London's largest. By the end of 1974 the new ticket hall was three-quarters complete, with the new escalator shafts well advanced. The steel deck was removed during the Easter weekend of 1975, and by the end of that year the first stage of the enlarged ticket hall area was complete apart from fitting out.

Before the enlarged ticket hall plans could be finished, the old part – still in use – had to be modernised and fully integrated, including modernisation of the 1920's escalators. To achieve this, a temporary ticket hall was created in the enlarged area and this was opened on 23rd January 1977, with a new entrance to the west of Davies Street. The new ticket hall had only temporary finishes, but the three new escalators were permanent enough and connected with new passages to the Central Line at the low level. The old ticket hall, together with the old Central Line escalators, closed the previous night and work began on clearing the area so that modernisation could proceed.

Phase 2 of the Bond Street reconstruction was completed at the end of 1978, when the temporary ticket hall was extended westwards, into the refurbished area which had been the old station; by now two replacement escalators had also been provided. The old and new lower escalator landings were also now linked. Although the majority of permanent features were now available, the full ticket hall area was still not ready and had to await completion of the shopping development on the former station site. This was ready the following year and provided an additional entrance, new escalators and ticket hall shopping area, though most of this was managed by the shopping centre and was technically outside the operating station.

Bond Street now had five escalators, and would gain three more when the Fleet Line opened; these would link the intermediate circulating area with the Fleet Line, which occupied the lowest level, the platforms flanking the lower concourse.

Green Park station had already been considerably enlarged for the Victoria Line, which had arrived there in 1969. Only comparatively minor works were needed at ticket hall level to accommodate the Fleet Line, mainly comprising an enlargement for a pair of escalators from the ticket hall to a new intermediate concourse. From here, two further escalators and a stairway were to lead to the Fleet Line platforms, and other new passages to the Victoria Line. Interchange with the Piccadilly Line was via a very long passageway here, and regulars soon got to know that it was less tiresome to use the escalators and go via ticket hall level.

The works at Green Park were comparatively simple, with most construction achieved through a working site in the park itself. By the end of 1974 the new upper flight of two escalators was being installed and the lower shaft was nearing completion, with escalators in hand the following year. (After the Line opened, rising traffic levels caused considerable congestion here, and on 1st November 1993 a third escalator was commissioned between the existing two, the stairway being replaced.)

At Strand, the new Fleet Line platforms were to have access both to the existing Trafalgar Square (Bakerloo) station and Strand (Northern) station. The works were comparatively minor at the former, confined in the main to an enlargement of the circulating area at the bottom of the existing pair of Bakerloo escalators. From here a new subway was to lead to three new escalators to the lower concourse, flanked by the new Fleet Line platforms. The existing Strand station was a remarkable survival from the Edwardian era. The existing cramped ticket hall with its original 1906 lifts was hopelessly inadequate and comprehensive enlargement and rebuilding was required. At Fleet Line concourse level, escalators (opposite those leading to the Bakerloo Line) would lead from the new platforms to an intermediate level which linked into the existing passages to the Northern Line; new escalators to the ticket hall also rose from this level. But there was now a difficulty. The optimal solution required the upper bank of three new escalators to pass through the line of the existing lift shafts, impossible while the station remained open. With temporary closure of the station inevitable, hardship was viewed as minor in view of the proximity of Trafalgar Square and Embankment stations.

The ticket hall area had to be increased very significantly, and the enlargement works required a steel deck to be erected over the forecourt of Charing Cross main line station. The first casualty of the works was the Villiers Street entrance to Strand which closed after traffic on 6th January 1973. Once preparatory work had been completed the deck itself was installed over the Easter weekend in April 1973.

Right **Poster showing remodelling of the Underground below Charing Cross.** LT Museum

How the new station combines the Jubilee, Northern and Bakerloo lines

LONDON'S GROWING UNDERGROUND

No: 5 JANUARY 1977 | THE NEW CHARING CROSS STATION

This artist's impression shows the general arrangement of the new Charing Cross Underground Station, now being built.

The new station complex will combine the former Strand (Northern Line) Station with the existing Trafalgar Square (Bakerloo Line) Station, adding a completely new station for the Fleet Line. The whole will provide three-line interchange with British Rail's Charing Cross terminus, with pedestrian subways linking the new Underground station with Villiers Street, Strand (north side) and Duncannon Street.

The work is being financed by the Government and the Greater London Council.

The Northern Line station itself closed after traffic on Saturday 16th June 1973, with publicity briefly, but optimistically, proclaiming a re-opening in 1976. The former lifts were speedily removed to allow the delicate work to proceed of building an escalator shaft diagonally down through the site of both lift shafts, work made even more complicated by the need to underpin the 300-ton Queen Eleanor memorial; this sat on top of the ticket hall extension and delayed these particular works from starting until 1974.

One major difficulty at Strand was lack of space to use as a working site, and a plot of land was used in the north-west corner of Trafalgar Square on which the National Gallery extension now stands. This required very lengthy temporary access passages to be built, linked both to the low-level station and new running tunnels. One passage bifurcated to link to Trafalgar Square station, with the other running to the bottom of the former Strand lifts; although not originally planned to do so, this 150-yard passage was eventually retained as a permanent interchange feature.

The lower escalator shafts were completed in 1974, and works at ticket hall level were sufficiently advanced the following year to allow the steel deck to be removed in November 1975, by which time the re-opening date was no longer being published – things had begun to slip badly, even though much of the ticket hall works were complete. By the end of 1977 the new subways (built by LT on behalf of the GLC as part of the works) were confidently expected the following year. The new Fleet Line substation was commissioned on 23rd December 1977, though with no railway to feed, its output was restricted to the supply of Trafalgar Square station, with which it was now linked via new subterranean passages (it was located in a new shaft near the Northern Line platforms at Strand). Beyond the new platforms the parliamentary powers were to be used to the full, with the running tunnels reaching as far as the Aldwych. In the interim the tunnels were to serve as over-runs and sidings.

For the enhanced services on the Stanmore branch, increased stabling accommodation was considered necessary, and it was decided to remodel the sidings at Stanmore, adjust the track layout and modernise the signalling – still of late 1930s origin. The seven sidings and reception road at Stanmore were thus taken out of commission from close of traffic Saturday night 16th June 1973, and the whole area was cleared. Ten new sidings and related trackwork were commissioned on 27th June 1976.

It was still necessary to provide the additional stabling space at Neasden Depot, which was only going to be released when Bakerloo Line maintenance was shifted to the new depot at Stonebridge Park. After a succession of delays the completion of the latter depot was marked by the commissioning of the control tower from Monday 26th March 1979 (after being postponed twice).

The decision relating to the supply of new trains for the Fleet Line was complicated by wider considerations. These partly related to the issue of the supply of new trains for the Underground at that time, a matter further influenced by a notoriously difficult period of service reliability. Uncertainty over the second and third stages of the Fleet Line made matters even more problematic. The outcome was to procure for Stage 1 of the Fleet Line a second batch of trains already in production for the Northern Line, and to introduce them by means of an inevitably complex cascade programme which would see them used on a number of lines at different times. The trains in question were called the 1972 Mk II stock, 33 in number, just sufficient for the Charing Cross–Stanmore service. They were similar but not identical to the 30 Mk I trains being introduced on the Northern Line, themselves based on the 1967 Victoria Line design but shortened to 7-cars and designed for 2-person manual operation.

At the time of ordering it was considered that the Fleet Line trains would be operated by one person, but with automatic train operation in use south of Finchley Road in order to meet what were then the Railway Inspectorate's safety requirements for one-person operation in single bore tube tunnels. The 1972 Mk II trains were thus fitted with door controls in the driving cabs and some provision for later conversion to automatic operation, including an 'auto' position on the driver's reversing switch turret.

As delivered they were fitted out for 2-person operation and were equipped with a conventional guard's position. This allowed them to enter service immediately on the Northern Line, releasing a substantial number of 1938 stock trains to be withdrawn; the first train entered service on 19th November 1973. Although similar to the Mk I trains which they ran alongside, there were some detail differences, including the fitting of motorised destination blinds linked to an electronic set number display; neither feature was at all satisfactory and both were replaced in due course, although they re-appeared later on new or refurbished trains in a more reliable form. Perhaps more prominently, the Mk II trains were fitted with red-painted passenger doors, beginning a trend which continues to this day.

In 1977 the Northern Line began to receive second-hand Piccadilly Line trains. This allowed withdrawal of the Northern's remaining 1938 stock, and the gradual transfer of the 1972 Mk IIs to the Bakerloo Line where they displaced the worst of its 1938 stock and operated alongside the rest; the first Mk II train ran on the Bakerloo Line on 4th April 1977 and initially the new trains generally operated on the Stanmore branch. The intention was that when the Fleet Line opened, the 1972 stock would be retained on the Stanmore (Fleet Line) service while refurbished 1938 stock remained on the Bakerloo. As a concession to Bakerloo Line staff who would otherwise have had to

Cars and units of 1972 MkII stock in Neasden Works. Maintenance is being carried out on the two cars in the foreground. John Glover

Car interior line diagrams for C stock trains were printed (but not used) showing Fleet Line interchange at Baker Street. The reprint with the change of name to Jubilee Line coincided with a change in representation of stations with British Rail interchange where their circles were given the same style as other interchange stations, with the arrows running through.

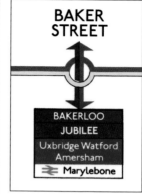

perform duty almost entirely in tunnel, both lines were to share the same train staff for some years after the new line opened (about half the Fleet Line mileage was in open air). Although some preliminary work was done the new line was not equipped for automatic operation when it opened, and 2-person operation with conventional signalling was used. Some additional modifications were made prior to service on the Bakerloo, including the fitting of train radio.

The year 1977 was Queen Elizabeth II's silver jubilee. It was also the year in which a new administration took charge at County Hall. The new leader of the Council was the redoubtable Horace Cutler, who, more or less upon taking office, proclaimed that the Fleet Line would henceforth be known as the 'Jubilee Line' in commemoration of the royal event. This development took LT a little by surprise as it had little forewarning but had to foot the £50,000 bill. The matter was also to become controversial and was formally opposed by the GLC's passenger's committee who felt that the money could be put to better use; in any case it preferred the name Fleet Line which was both established and had geographical links, as the plans then stood. Nor was the line expected to open until 1978, and it would certainly miss jubilee year. The Council sought belatedly to explain its position by suggesting that 'while the name has no geographical links, the jubilee is an event of such importance to deserve commemoration, and that the renaming of a new Underground line is a fitting and striking way for London to do so'. 'The cost of £50,000 is not excessive in comparative terms, and might well be viewed in the context of the extra tourist trade the silver jubilee has brought to London this year'. In any case LT had perforce to put the changes in hand prior to getting a formal direction from the GLC in September, who observed it would be 'confusing' to change it back again. So Jubilee Line it became – within LT the change was announced in August. Subsequent events, which saw the Fleet Street routeing jettisoned, may on reflection mean the name change turned out for the best.

Progress on most aspects of the Jubilee Line had been good, particularly the major civil engineering works. It was not so good in the electrical and mechanical fitting out. As early as the end of 1975 a start had been made on the line's architectural work and on the installation of equipment. A year later progress had been a little slower than hoped but it was still envisaged the whole line would open in 1978: this was to prove optimistic. During 1977 it was admitted serious delays were occurring, especially in relation to the installation of escalators, where industrial relations problems at the contractors had not helped. Nevertheless a 1978 opening date was still anticipated, even if it were only at the end of the year. But by the end of 1978 things were still far from complete with regard to the fitting out of stations, notably at Charing Cross, where unfinished escalators continued to delay matters.

The Jubilee Line tracks, signalling and control systems were commissioned from Monday 14th August 1978 so that trial running could begin. Power was supplied from Baker Street substation and new ones at Charing Cross and Hays Mews (north of Green Park). The latter sat atop a former working shaft which during construction had been encased within a sound-proofed structure to avoid disturbing the local residents; the substation itself was designed to blend in with the local surroundings. Fanshafts were commissioned at Lisson Green, Park Square Gardens, Hays Mews and Southampton Street.

Signalling at Charing Cross was arranged to operate automatically by means of programme machines, where a punched roll containing the timetable operated the interlocking equipment. It was supervised by the signalman (styled regulator) at Finchley Road cabin where additional equipment was provided by which means the Charing Cross signalling could also be operated by push-button control. The signalling at Baker Street had already been similarly updated in 1977.

Although automatic train operation was not provided for at this time, it did remain a long-term aspiration, and some further development work was undertaken. However, by now thoughts were turning to its application on the 'final' stock for the Jubilee Line whose arrival was anticipated about 1984, when further stages of the Line had been built. The 1972 Mk II trains would then be transferred to the Bakerloo (probably still in 2-person operation mode) to replace the last of the 1938 stock.

The Jubilee Line opened to the public on 1st May 1979, following the official ceremony on the previous day. The formalities were undertaken by HRH Prince Charles, Prince of Wales, who travelled by train from Green Park to Charing Cross (where the ceremony took place) and thence to Stanmore.

A few days before the official opening of the Jubilee Line, an unusual reception was given at Bond Street station by Phillips, the nearby fine art auctioneers. A string quartet entertains guests and staff. Daily Telegraph

When the public arrived they found the finishes at the three new stations followed a common design theme which consisted of a white melamine-panelled ceiling and tiled walls with the usual station features (such as station names and litter bins) in moulded plastic units. Charing Cross had plain green tiles with images of Nelson depicted on a white ground behind the seats. Green Park (perhaps confusingly) adopted red tiles with a leaf design. At Bond Street the tiling was predominantly bright blue with a 'shopping package' design providing relief. At Baker Street the Jubilee platforms were largely red, but pictorial display areas were given over to images based on the Sherlock Holmes stories. Other parts of the stations were modernised as elements of separate packages of work, and had their own themes.

Left **The enlarged booking hall at Charing Cross opened at the time of the start of Jubilee Line services in May 1979.**
Capital Transport

Below **Baker Street platform showing one of the Sherlock Holmes drawings.**
Capital Transport

Stations south of Baker Street on the original Jubilee Line were distinguished by the tile colour and motifs as shown in these photographs. As a fire precaution the white melamine ceiling panelling was later replaced at Baker Street, Bond Street and Green Park by fire retarding material. Shown here are Bond Street, Green Park and Charing Cross.
Capital Transport

On the same day the Jubilee Line came into use, some other necessary adjustments were made to familiar names on the Underground diagram. Strand station on the Northern Line re-opened at the same time, and Trafalgar Square on the Bakerloo was incorporated into the same station complex. It was concluded that the station could only have one name, so the whole lot was renamed Charing Cross – a name in any case which Strand had had until 1914. A major complication was the existing Charing Cross Underground station, just down the road, which served the Northern, Bakerloo and District Lines. To mitigate the inevitable confusion the existing Charing Cross station

One of the neat information kiosks at each end of the forecourt at Stanmore dating back to early LT days. Taken just before the line transferred to the Jubilee in 1979, a relevant poster is visible.
Capital Transport

was renamed Charing Cross (Embankment) on 4th August 1974 so that people could get used to the new way of things, and simply to Embankment on 12th September 1976, which left the old name clear for the Jubilee Line station.

Trafalgar Square Bakerloo Line platforms, now a part of the Jubilee Line station complex, also became 'Charing Cross' from 1st May 1979, though the platforms remained in their Edwardian form for a couple more years until bright and colourful new surfaces were installed based on National Gallery works of art. The Northern Line platforms, however, were completely refurbished from re-opening and incorporated surfaces bearing images relating to the construction of Queen Eleanor's Cross.

The arrival of the Jubilee Line created an immediate improvement in train service levels. In the morning peak the number of departures from Stanmore remained at 15 trains, but a further eight trains were introduced from the intermediate reversing points at Wembley Park, Willesden Green or West Hampstead. South of West Hampstead intervals were now at 2½-3 minutes, instead of 4 hitherto. Evening peak improvements were similar, although there were no West Hampstead reversers. Off-peak improvements were also made. During the mid-day period, for example a 6-minute interval service to Wembley Park (12 minutes to Stanmore), gave way to a 3½- to 4-minute interval to Willesden Green, 3½-7½ minutes to Wembley Park, and 7½ minutes to Stanmore.

The cost of Stage 1 eventually came out as £90m (worth some £250-300m at today's prices). However it soon achieved one of its major objectives – within six months very nearly half the passengers on the Bakerloo's bottleneck section south of Baker Street had transferred to the Jubilee, whilst north of Baker Street Jubilee traffic had already reached ten per cent growth. Comparable improvements were made to Bakerloo services, and traffic north-west of Baker Street also developed as a result.

Considerable publicity surrounded the inauguration of the Jubilee Line in 1979. The 'All Change' poster was intended to get Stanmore branch passengers used to the new name.
Capital Transport

49

Docklands and the River Line

At the end of 1972, with Stage 1 of the new railway now in hand, LT was still pressing for authority to get on with Stage 2. It argued that Stage 2 would still be needed as far as Fenchurch Street whatever the outcome of the Docklands study and that the line would bring early relief to a number of pinch points. By the end of 1973 things looked more gloomy in the face of impending government spending cuts. LT pointed out how inappropriate a terminus Charing Cross would be for any length of time and it commissioned its own study into the benefits the line would bring to south-east London. But there was by now a new distraction. A study into future railway developments in London, the 'London Rail Study', had been commissioned in February 1973 and the government was clear that no authorisation would be given to LT for any new railway until that study had reported, which would not be until at least mid-1974.

The key government report into the potential regeneration of the Docklands area was published in January 1973. The conclusions it reached about the potential for release of development land from (mainly) the Port of London Authority and the Gas Corporation proved fairly accurate in the circumstances, even if other assumptions were to go a little off the mark (though perhaps only with the benefit of hindsight). The study identified that whilst the tonnage of cargo handled at the upstream docks as a whole had remained relatively static, the handling was being achieved through a rapidly diminishing number of quays. For all sorts of reasons the implication was that there would become a time when the whole docks traffic could be handled most efficiently further downstream, particularly at Tilbury. Already the number of docks had been rationalised: East India Dock closed in 1967, St Katherine Dock in 1968, Surrey Docks in 1970, with numerous berths at other docks closed. The report suggested that the West India and Millwall docks would close by 1978, Poplar Dock and most of the Royal Victoria Dock by around 1983, and the rest of the Royal Docks by around 1988. The Gas Corporation land at Beckton and on the Greenwich Peninsula, much of which was already derelict, also seemed to have a limited future with the arrival of natural gas.

In transport terms the area was awkward, being roughly 10 km by 2km and with the Thames meandering through it, dividing it into separate halves with very little communication between the two. Roads and railways were principally arranged for goods transport to and from the docks and were at least in part unsuitable for new types of development. The river was viewed as a major obstruction and a number of new river crossings were thought essential (the option of moving the river was also looked at). New transport infrastructure was viewed as critical for regeneration and some sort of 'rapid transit' link was proposed. To be effective this had to serve the whole area, yet be linked to the Underground network somewhere; a bus option was also investigated but was not favoured. The consultants proposed a routeing from Fenchurch Street via Surrey Docks, Isle of Dogs, Greenwich Peninsula, Custom House, Beckton and Barking, with a branch from Custom House to Woolwich and Thamesmead; a couple of detailed routeing options were offered. Significantly, it was felt that the traffic potential would not be likely to warrant tube railway 'heavy rail'

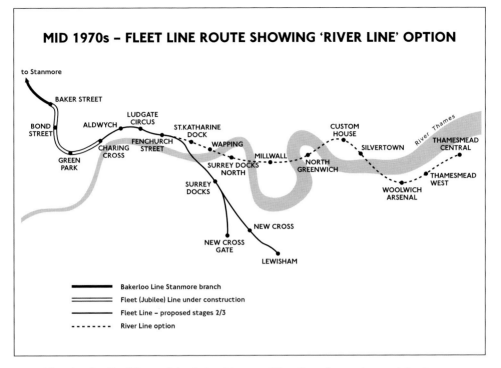

MID 1970s – FLEET LINE ROUTE SHOWING 'RIVER LINE' OPTION

to Stanmore

BAKER STREET

LUDGATE
CIRCUS
BOND   ALDWYCH   ST.KATHARINE   CUSTOM
STREET   DOCK   HOUSE
       FENCHURCH   WAPPING   SILVERTOWN
CHARING   STREET
GREEN   CROSS   MILLWALL
PARK   SURREY DOCKS   NORTH
            NORTH   GREENWICH

THAMESMEAD
CENTRAL

THAMESMEAD
WEST
WOOLWICH
ARSENAL

SURREY
DOCKS

River Thames

NEW CROSS

NEW CROSS
GATE

LEWISHAM

▬▬▬ Bakerloo Line Stanmore branch
═══ Fleet (Jubilee) Line under construction
─── Fleet Line – proposed stages 2/3
- - - - - River Line option

Map showing Fleet Line routeing to Lewisham and the alternative eastern routeing to Thamesmead – styled the River Line. Designed to render the Docklands redevelopment zone much more accessible, the River Line's many Thames crossings were a valuable feature adopted by the Jubilee Line extension as built.

technology and some form of mini-tram was proposed. In any event a marker had been put down that some sort of rapid transit system running through the Docklands 'spine', and with multiple river crossings, was important to regeneration of the area.

The London Rail Study was eventually published in November 1974, prior to which LT could make little progress other than to lobby hard. The study acknowledged the benefit of a 'spinal' rapid transit route through Docklands and proposed a route to Thamesmead very similar to that put forward in the Docklands study eighteen months earlier, but without the Beckton branch. It considered that a tube railway would be more appropriate than a light rail system, and that it should take the form of an extension of the Fleet Line (for descriptive purposes the Docklands route east of Fenchurch Street was termed 'River Line', but it was never to be a separate railway). An alternative proposal for the Fleet Line was retention of the Lewisham objective, but with a further extension over BR tracks to Addiscombe and Hayes to relieve those branches. Notwithstanding continued interest in the Lewisham option it was observed that conditions had changed since LT and BR had originally proposed it, and the need was now somewhat less pressing. On balance the preference was for the Fleet Line to go to Thamesmead via Docklands. In any event the study was (with some irony) keen to see an early start to Fleet Line Stage 2 (to the City), a matter LT picked up on very quickly.

A year later LT was still pressing vigorously for the money for Stage 2. The Department of the Environment (DoE) maintained with equal vigour that Stage 2 could not be justified without certainty of developments beyond. But developments beyond to a significant extent depended on effective transport provision, and that now hinged on the nature and timing of the regeneration programme, to which ends a strategic plan was now in hand. This was expected sometime in 1976, following which 'decisions on the Underground would be needed, in the context of other transport priorities for Docklands'. In fact the London Docklands Strategic Plan was completed in July 1976. This reiterated earlier support for a west-east tube with other complementary improvements, and was heavily supported. LT continued to press for a 'River Line' routeing to Thamesmead via Millwall, Silvertown and Woolwich, but there was significant alternative pressure for a Thamesmead via Beckton route; it was considered sufficient to make provision for a shuttle service from Custom House to Beckton, whilst not ruling out through trains in the longer term (especially as a depot was proposed at Beckton). By the end of 1976 detailed 'River Line' planning work was in hand with a view to seeking powers in 1978 for the section between Fenchurch Street and Custom House, with powers for the rest of the line to be sought the following year. But there was still no move towards constructing Stage 2 as far as Fenchurch Street.

Planning proceeded during 1977, during which year consideration was given to the building of a single bore of the under-river rail tunnels from Woolwich to Custom House in advance of any authorisation for extension of the Jubilee Line (as it was now called). It was anticipated that this could temporarily become part of the BR North London Line service, or at least connect into it. As a precautionary measure the former 'Stage 3' powers for the Fenchurch Street–New Cross section were renewed during the year, though for practical purposes this alignment was dead.

1978 was a little more eventful. LT lodged a bill for construction of the Fenchurch Street–Woolwich section of line (including the Beckton branch). Further delay to this evidently ill-fated extension arose because parliament was dissolved in April 1979 for the general election, causing the bill a year's delay: the Royal Assent was not granted until 1st August 1980. At the GLC's request detailed plans for early construction of the Woolwich tunnel section were pushed forward, but of course nothing could be done without the powers. But the GLC's formidable Horace Cutler was determined to show that something could be done. Amidst much publicity he travelled to Aldwych on 4th May 1978 to launch the beginning of a 3-month programme of exploratory works on the site of Aldwych Jubilee Line station near St Clement Danes church. Hailed as the start of the construction of the Jubilee Line extension these works were really only a necessary preliminary to the construction of the planned 'umbrella' bridge over the ticket hall site, which was expected to be the longest and most critical job on Stage 2. The exploration cost just £50,000, but Cutler showed his frustration at the continued lack of government support and made it clear that the GLC was determined to go ahead and was even prepared to pay for the line – from the rates, if necessary.

In June 1979 matters were to take a significant new turn. Horrified by the spiralling cost of a full-blown Jubilee Line extension (now estimated at £325m), the new government persuaded the GLC to agree to examine lower cost options, and a new report was undertaken. Whilst this was in hand LT decided not at that stage to seek powers for the Woolwich to Thamesmead section, although planning for the construction of the single-bore tube tunnel under the river continued. The Low Cost Options report was completed early in 1980 and drew attention to five principal options:

A City Corporation notice at a site at the foot of Ludgate Hill reserved for the planned station here when the extension to Fenchurch Street and beyond was being safeguarded.

◇ a dedicated busway from Beckton to Canning Town, with express buses projected through to Aldgate East, including a loop serving the Isle of Dogs (£15m);

◇ a dedicated busway from Beckton to Stepney (including a loop serving the Isle of Dogs using normal roads) then normal roads to Aldgate East (£24m);

◇ a street tramway from Beckton to Aldgate East, some of it on dedicated tracks (£40–£60m);

◇ an Automated Light Rapid Transit (ALRT) system (considered highly radical) on dedicated tracks from Aldgate East to Beckton, with a branch from West India Docks to North Greenwich (£120m);

◇ or an 'interim' Jubilee Line extension from Charing Cross to Beckton, but omitting the Thamesmead branch and any stations at Aldwych, Ludgate Circus, St Katharine Dock and part of Cannon Street (£200m).

These proposals all compared favourably with the £325m for the complete Jubilee Line extension, though all had significantly lesser benefits.

The immediate outcome of the report was that the government decided to channel the available transport funding for Docklands improvements into roads, and a Jubilee Line extension (at least in the form described) was to wither and die. LT sought to maintain the pressure for a while longer and quietly and correctly concluded that if the Docklands redevelopment really did take off a tube railway would be justified.

Although not built, the cost of stage 2 was not insignificant. Quite apart from all the abortive planning work, and the cost of obtaining parliamentary powers, there was the expensive issue of 'safeguarding'. It was hard enough to find a route through the City which avoided the deep foundations of modern buildings, but such a route was not easy to preserve. Landowners could not be expected to desist from development plans indefinitely because of an aspirational railway, nor could some 'blighted' sites carry on indefinitely. The result was that around £10m was eventually spent on protective works for stage 2, and it might easily have been very much more. The subsoil was purchased and at one point LT actually considered building the empty tunnels as the cheapest protective option.

This is no place to chart the history of the Docklands Light Railway (DLR), but suffice to say that a study in 1981 endorsed construction of such a line along a very similar routeing to the ALRT line already described, but initially without the Beckton section; a separate branch from the West India Docks to Stratford was also incorporated, and the entire project was capped at £77m. Funding came jointly from the Departments of Transport and the Environment, channelled through the newly formed London Docklands Development Corporation, who viewed the railway as critical to get developers on board. LT obtained construction powers in 1984-5, with the line opening on 30th July 1987 (by which time powers to extend to Beckton had been obtained). Temporarily, it seemed, transport needs in Docklands were to be met, but for the reasons below they were not to be met satisfactorily.

In 1985 a proposal emerged for a major new development on the Isle of Dogs. This was partly precipitated by the lack of space within the City of London for new development sites for the banks, and the apparent advantages of adopting a vast and nearby 'brown-field' site – provided one could get there. Thought to be the largest construction project in Europe, the developer planned a 1½ million square metre complex of offices, retail and leisure facilities on the larger of the central dock quays within the West India Dock – more familiarly known as the Canary Wharf. The difficulty was that the Development Corporation's planning regime would permit this welcome development even though the planned infrastructure would clearly be unable to support it – the DLR was only designed with an installed daily capacity of under 30,000 journeys, whilst the Canary Wharf development alone would potentially introduce an additional 50,000 jobs. The DLR would almost certainly be heavily overloaded. Nevertheless, Canary Wharf's promoter (a Texan called G. Ware Travelstead) persuaded the government to offer support to a significantly upgraded transport infrastructure, to which it acquiesced on the basis of not having to bear significant cost.

An early outcome was a decision to upgrade the DLR (which could not be done until after it had opened) and to construct a DLR link to Bank Underground station, considerably improving interchange facilities. The DLR improvements heralded an interesting new form of partnership which set the tone for the future. The government (through LT) provided the political support, but the private sector contributed some £70m towards the DLR upgrading costs, reflecting the importance the Canary Wharf promoters placed upon efficient public transport to their otherwise somewhat remote new 'city'. As a separate matter the DLR was also extended from Poplar to Beckton via the Royal Docks, completing the provision of a mass transit system along the original Docklands spine. Although the expanded DLR was expected to cope (just) with the first phase of the Canary Wharf development, it was still unrealistic to expect it to address the additional traffic created by the second phase, and without sufficient transport infrastructure it was difficult to see how the second phase could proceed. The expanded DLR was expected to cope with 65,000 passengers daily, but with jobs elsewhere in the vicinity of the DLR increasing at a phenomenal rate, Canary Wharf phase 2 could still not realistically proceed.

By this time Travelstead's increasingly nervous consortium had sold out to Canadian developers Olympia & York, who continued the pressure to see what could be done to make radical improvements to the transport infrastructure, including extension of the DLR to Lewisham and a further railway line. But the weight of opinion was that comparatively minor improvements would neither unlock the capacity needed, nor improve journey times to key interchanges and provide an adequate choice of routes. All logic pointed to a heavy rail solution.

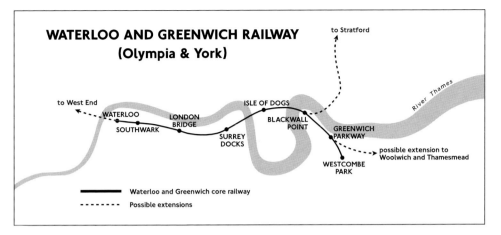

WATERLOO AND GREENWICH RAILWAY
(Olympia & York)

to Stratford

to West End

WATERLOO
SOUTHWARK
LONDON BRIDGE
SURREY DOCKS
ISLE OF DOGS
BLACKWALL POINT
GREENWICH PARKWAY
WESTCOMBE PARK
River Thames

possible extension to
Woolwich and Thamesmead

▬▬▬▬ Waterloo and Greenwich core railway
- - - - - - - Possible extensions

Map showing the planned routeing of the Waterloo & Greenwich Railway promoted by Olympia & York. The section from Waterloo to Blackwall Point (and thence towards Stratford) forms the current route of the extended Jubilee Line with 'Isle of Dogs' becoming 'Canary Wharf', and 'Blackwall Point' becoming 'North Greenwich', a station with provision for a future junction with a branch towards Thamesmead.

And so it was that Olympia & York pushed for the construction of a new heavy rail link between Canary Wharf and Waterloo, via London Bridge. Initially consideration was given to the extension of the Bakerloo Line to Canary Wharf, either from Elephant & Castle or direct from Waterloo, and with the possibility of a northerly extension beyond Canary Wharf to Stratford or Tottenham, and with the option of a branch to the Royal Docks. In the event a Bakerloo extension was not considered feasible.

In due course a dedicated route – the Waterloo & Greenwich Railway – seemed to be the most realistic option. Starting at Waterloo it would have run via Southwark, London Bridge, Surrey Quays, Canary Wharf, and on to a depot site at Westcombe Park with additional stations at Blackwall Point and Greenwich Parkway (both on the Greenwich peninsula). The railway, though self-contained, was considered suitable for extension at each end, perhaps to Paddington in the west and with a branch from Blackwall Point to Stratford in the east.

Olympia & York and LT began jointly to plan the Waterloo & Greenwich Railway, and put a proposal to government in autumn 1988. It would not be cheap. This was the first major proposal for an underground railway put forward since the disastrous fire at King's Cross in 1987, and comprehensively more stringent safety arrangements were required, including expensive large diameter tunnels and many more facilities at stations. With overall efficiency further reduced by the comparatively short point-to-point route, the railway failed to offer by some way the necessary social cost-benefit which would meet the usual criteria for government funding. LT considered that the case could be improved by linking the railway to the Jubilee Line, and to extend northwards to Stratford to tap the east and north-easterly transport corridors, thus generating significant networkwide social benefits. Olympia & York became impatient and pressed for a stand-alone Waterloo & Greenwich railway bill to be deposited in November 1988. LT, who had more experience in such matters, were convinced the timing was poor as yet another rail study was imminent and all experience thus far suggested that unsupported bills under such circumstances could not make progress.

A Jubilee Line extension emerges

In parallel with the mounting concern about transport access to Docklands there was increasing political agitation for the construction of other new railway lines in London; the outcome was a study team being established to consider both existing and new proposals. The team consisted of representatives from the Department of Transport, British Rail Network SouthEast, London Transport and London Underground Limited (a subsidiary of LT created in 1985 to manage the Underground). The report, called the Central London Rail Study, was published in January 1989.

Amongst the various proposals for new lines the report envisaged the extension of the Jubilee Line east of Charing Cross. One option contemplated an extension via Aldwych and the City to Liverpool Street and Whitechapel, and perhaps beyond to Stratford and Ilford to afford relief to the overcrowded section of the Great Eastern main line. Good interchange was envisaged with the District and East London lines at Whitechapel and with the Central Line at Stratford. Another possible option was to divert the Jubilee Line parallel to the Central Line as far as Leytonstone and take over the southern part of the Hainault Loop, allowing Central Line services to be strengthened on the Epping branch.

Another possibility was to extend the Jubilee Line through to the City and then to divert southwards to a terminus beneath London Bridge station. It was observed that such a choice of route would allow subsequent extension towards the Docklands area or a possible link to the privately promoted tube railway between Canary Wharf and Waterloo which also was to pass through London Bridge. Such possible routeings would be the subject of a further study into possible East London rail improvements which was to follow shortly.

Both the above schemes were weaker than others in respect of relieving the Central Line corridor (Crossrail – a full sized central London tube based on the Paris RER – was by comparison a very strong option). The report did not dismiss the option of sending the Jubilee Line to Docklands along the Olympia & York route. That, however, was outside the remit of a central London study, so all that could be done was to recommend further evaluation work.

The result was an East London Rail study with a remit to identify: 'the best option for further improving rail access from central London to Docklands and East Thames-side in order to accommodate the rapid pace of developments in Docklands.' It emerged in September 1989 (the main findings were known in July), having considered all manner of possible options and variations. The key conclusion was a preferred option for the Jubilee Line to be extended from Green Park to Stratford, adopting the route of the Waterloo and Greenwich railway en route. Two options were offered for the Canary Wharf–Canning Town section, one via North Greenwich, involving two river crossings, and the other via Brunswick, keeping to the north bank. Other matters were left for further possible evaluation, including sharing the existing North London Line tracks to Stratford, and a westerly extension to Paddington: suffice to say neither was pursued with much vigour.

Naturally the proposed routeing from Green Park to Waterloo via Westminster proved controversial, not least because it implied abandoning the Green Park–Charing Cross section completed only ten years earlier, but all options had been examined. A routeing from Charing Cross to Canada Water via Fleet Street would have cost much the same as one via Waterloo and delivered comparable traffic flows. However the route partly duplicated the District and Circle lines while the more southerly route opened up new areas and was much preferred on planning grounds. Perhaps even more importantly the developers had a very much stronger preference for a direct route to Waterloo and London Bridge, simplifying journeys to Canary Wharf from the stockbroker belt.

Given the preference for a Waterloo routeing, the next issue was whether or not this could be achieved by utilising the infrastructure at Charing Cross, not itself far from Waterloo but running at right angles to the Waterloo–London Bridge alignment. The short answer was that this could not be done without sharp reverse curves, and the disbenefits of speed restrictions and excess running times meant that a direct route from Green Park was more worthwhile given the comparatively light usage of Charing Cross (Jubilee) and the easy alternative routes. The only remaining question was whether the link should serve Embankment, St James's Park or Westminster; the latter was favoured for several reasons and it was the most direct.

Regarding the report as a most encouraging development a joint LT/LUL/O&Y team was able to submit the necessary but hurried private bill in November 1989, with O&Y contributing to the costs of preparation. In parallel, considerable further work was undertaken to finalise the overall design. This further design work inevitably caused some changes to be required to the route put forward in the 1989 bill, including (in early 1990) a switch of route from the Brunswick Wharf option to that via North Greenwich, precipitated by a stated willingness of British Gas to contribute to the funding as a consequence of the inevitable increase in land price which would result. The outcome was a further bill, deposited in November 1990, containing the necessary alterations. Parliament decided to consolidate the bills and address them as one. After due consideration it received the Royal Assent on 16th March 1992 as the London Transport Act 1992. Despite some heavy petitioning against the scheme, the original intentions came through comparatively unscathed.

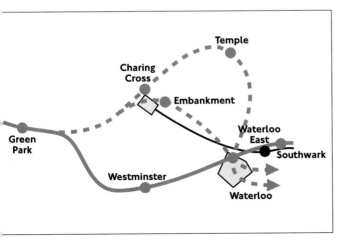

Map of the alternative ways considered of connecting the original Jubilee Line with Waterloo and Docklands. Sharp curves ruled out the Charing Cross option.

The cost of new deep tube railway schemes is now truly phenomenal, with £1000m plus representing only a comparatively modest result. But in government funding terms it represents massive forward commitment – once construction has started the funding can hardly be switched off. In consequence, the government in the early'nineties was not prepared to fund two such railway schemes at the same time. Its initially favoured scheme was CrossRail, which offered major benefits to central London and some useful outer suburban destinations on British Rail; furthermore a project team had worked up a deliverable scheme over some years. On the other hand it was vital to support Canary Wharf, and the economy it was looking to rejuvenate. It could not do both. In the end the partly constructed and very visible Canary Wharf development gained the vital support, subject to some essential external funding. CrossRail had to go on the back burner.

Even with the considerable social benefits the Jubilee Line extension would bring, the overall case for public funding was somewhat marginal. Construction cost by this stage was expected to be in the region of £1300m – more than three times the cost of the London & Greenwich proposal. Olympia & York would inevitably be the principal beneficiary since the Canary Wharf development could not succeed without the necessary public transport infrastructure. For this reason the developer agreed to contribute some £400m to the Jubilee Line scheme, spread across several years. In addition there was the further £25m from British Gas. These contributions were said to be central to the receipt of government support. On the other hand other developers – who equally expected to enjoy the benefits – were less keen to contribute, presumably (and correctly) surmising that the O&Y offering would be sufficient to make the case without the need to dip into their own pockets, particularly in the face of recession. In the event the emerging political imperative for the line meant the government was content to accept the O&Y contributions over a surprisingly long 20-year period, very significantly reducing the value of the money (in money value terms the contribution amounted roundly to only a seventh of the cost instead of a third if it had been paid up front).

Regrettably, it was this very face of recession to which Olympia & York itself fell victim. They were not only unable to make their first payment to LT in April 1992, but went into administration in May. Without their contribution the government – hardened by its own financial difficulties – refused to sanction construction. The scheme was on ice. The only solution was to find a new source of private sector funding, achieved only after 18 months of difficult negotiation. Despite the recession there was sufficient confidence (and heavy investment already) to keep the Canary Wharf concept alive. The development vehicle, Canary Wharf Limited, was now owned by a consortium of 11 banks – some of whom stood to lose considerable money if the development failed. Fortunately the banks were finally persuaded that the development's success could only be achieved with efficient public transport.

LT and the government remained ready to move. Canary Wharf Limited emerged from administration on 29th October 1993 and within hours the Secretary of State for Transport signed a letter of authority allowing London Underground to proceed with the extension on the basis of an initial private sector contribution of £98m (from the European Investment Bank), with the balance of the £400m being contributed over 25 years following the opening. Receipt of the letter by LT's Chairman released letters of acceptance for the first of the construction contracts, and within a week contracts to the value of £900m had been let, with site works expected to begin about a month later. In early December, construction work began.

To maintain confidence in an imminent arrival of the Jubilee Line a single carriage was borrowed from the manufacturers and displayed in Cabot Square (Canary Wharf) from 29th to 31st May 1996, somewhat in advance of fleet delivery. Mike Horne

By this time construction costs had risen to £1900m, partly reflecting the inevitable cost rises during the delay and firmer prices following on-going design and site investigation, but also by inclusion of a completely new fleet of trains rather than making do partly with existing ones.

Prior to talk of an extension, signalling between Baker Street and Canons Park had been completely modernised during 1984-85, replacing that installed between 1937 and 1954. At reversing points and junctions new remotely controlled interlocking machines were provided although control itself was retained by signalmen in the existing signal cabins; the signal frame at Finchley Road was superseded by a temporary push-button control panel, but at Willesden Green the existing frame, and at Wembley Park the existing control desk, were temporarily adapted.

The re-signalling was a prelude to the transfer of local control to a new integrated computerised control centre at Baker Street, which would eventually supervise all train movements between Aldgate and Wembley Park on the Metropolitan Line, and Charing Cross and Stanmore on the Jubilee. The control room opened on 25th October 1986, with operation of the Stanmore interlocking transferred to the new facility. Charing Cross–Baker Street followed on 30th November 1986 with control transferred from the signal box at Finchley Road. West Hampstead and Finchley Road itself were transferred on 18th January 1987 with Willesden Green following on 1st February 1987 and Wembley Park signal box on 12th April 1987, completing this phase of the exercise.

For another year the signal boxes at Neasden (North and South) were retained to control movements to and from the depot. From 16th October 1988 these were replaced by a depot control room which controlled all train movements within the depot, ground signals and track circuits having been universally provided outside the sheds, and the points motorised. Interlocking was achieved by means of a new computerised interlocking arrangement, intended as much as anything else to test on a comprehensive scale its reliability prior to further possible use on the Underground.

Jubilee Line trains

It had always been thought that the 1972 MkII trains would have a short life on the Jubilee Line. In due course a completely new fleet of about 60 trains would be needed when Stages 2 and 3 were authorised; this would allow the 33 MkII trains to be cascaded to the Bakerloo Line – which conveniently required a similar total number of trains – and in turn replace the last of the 1938 stock which would be scrapped. Design work for the new trains proceeded accordingly.

But we have already seen that the Jubilee Line stages 2 and 3 never happened. The delay and indecision began to create havoc with the planned rolling stock cascade, and the 1938 stock on the Bakerloo became increasingly and unacceptably unreliable. Something had to be done. It was therefore decided in May 1982 to order a mere 15 trains of new stock (known as 1983 stock) which would allow the worst of the 1938 stock to be disposed of. The new trains, ordered from Metro Cammell in Birmingham, were formed into two identical 3-car units, and the first 6-car train entered service on 2nd May 1984.

However, this move was overtaken by events. Towards the end of 1982 London Transport was obliged to make significant service reductions following a dip in passenger numbers; in the wake of this it became possible to re-allocate spare trains. Thus the Bakerloo Line received 15 (later 16) 1959 stock trains from the Northern Line, allowing the worst of the 1938 stock to be withdrawn sooner than planned; as part of this re-allocation programme four 1972 MkII trains were transferred from the Jubilee back to the Northern Line early in 1983. When the 1983 stock trains entered service 14 more trains of 1972 MkII stock were transferred from the Jubilee to the Northern, with consequential moves resulting in the demise of the 1938 stock from the Bakerloo.

The 1983 stock comprised only two types of car, driving motors and trailers. It was to be unique in modern rolling stock history in being the only tube stock to be fitted entirely with single-leaf doorways, although they had been used on the sub-surface 'D' stock, with mixed reception. Although the doors in the centre of the cars were wider than normal single-leaf doors, they were not as wide as a traditional double-door, and the outcome was that boarding times tended to be prolonged unduly when traffic was heavy; the advantage was mainly in reduced maintenance. They were the first modern tube stock trains to re-introduce passenger-operated push-button door controls, this time mandatory at all stations, though still under the overriding control of train staff. Each car was longer than a 1972 car, so overall train lengths were similar. All cars seated 48 passengers, the seating capacity per train being 288, comparing favourably with 264 on a 7-car train of 1972 stock.

It was perhaps inevitable that train services would gradually need to drift back to pre-1982 levels, the outcome of which was a shortage of trains. This resulted in a decision in 1986 to order a further 16½ trains of 1983 stock (called 1983 MkII stock) to redress the balance. These were similar to the initial MkI batch but contained a number of detailed differences. The first entered service on the Jubilee Line on 27th November

A 1983 stock train at Charing Cross when new. LT Museum

1987, following which the remaining 1972 MkII trains ended up on the Bakerloo (achieving the original objective of the Bakerloo being entirely populated by 1972 stock).

Available for service the following year were three 4-car experimental trains built by different manufacturers as a trial for a proposed new fleet for the Central Line, but tested on the Jubilee. Two of the trains (Red and Green) were built by Metro-Cammell (now Alstom), and the third (Blue) was built by BREL (now AdTranz). The units were interchangeable and could form two 6-car trains which mainly ran as additional to the regular timetable. Much useful experience was gained from these somewhat unreliable units, which were finally withdrawn after one of them disgraced itself in a major derailment near Neasden in September 1989.

When the Jubilee Line was born in 1979, it was still vaguely the intention to install a system of automatic train operation, for which some provision had been made on the trains and to a lesser extent the trackside equipment; indeed one train was initially set aside for the development work. Automatic train operation (ATO) did not happen. Reasons included uncertainty over the future of the line, difficult to justify expense, a change in the rolling stock allocation policy and perhaps most importantly a relaxation of the Railway Inspectorate's rules which looked set to allow one-person operation of trains in deep-level tube tunnels subject to various safety requirements being met. In consequence one-person operation was introduced on 28th March 1988, with various modifications being made to the rolling stock beforehand, for example door controls duplicated in the driving cabs. Full automation would now have to wait for the line to be extended.

A depressing outcome to the final decision to go ahead with a Jubilee Line extension was the complete withdrawal of the 1983 stock. There was understandable reluctance to consign to the scrap-heap trains half of which were only ten or so years old, and the rest still under half-life, so naturally a host of options were considered. The stock was not popular, with its slow boarding times and indifferent reliability levels, so there was no enthusiasm at all either for building more of the trains or for running them in tandem with a similar number of 'new generation' trains, whose performance would have needed to be factored down to match. A further complication was the presence of quantities of no-longer compliant internal materials, requiring expensive removal to meet the latest fire resistance standards. A serious option was to rebuild at least some of the 1983 stock cars and infiltrate them into about 60 new trains made up also of new generation cars. This too was not proceeded with, mainly on grounds of cost, and in the event 59 completely new trains were ordered. The bulk of the 1983 stock was therefore scrapped, but a number of MkII units were retained to supplement the train service on the Piccadilly Line.

With authorisation of the Jubilee Line extension, the new trains were high on the agenda for attention – at over £250m they represented the largest single contract. The car bodies and assembly were entrusted to GEC Alsthom (now Alstom), who had taken over Metro-Cammell's Washwood Heath plant near Birmingham, where the bodies were assembled. Car bodies were built in Barcelona in extruded aluminium sections and shipped ready painted to the UK; the externally hung doors came from Canada and the 'H' frame bogies came from France.

Each train was of six cars comprising two 3-car units. Each unit consisted of a driving

A 1992 design for the front of the new trains. Trevor Scott Associates

motor car at one end, a motor car at the other end with a coupling point and 'shunting' control panel, and a trailer between them; each motor car was equipped with four 3-phase a.c. traction motors supplied by a thyristor inverter unit using 'gate turn-off' technology supplied by the usual 630 volt line current – these are the first LUL trains to use this lighter and comparatively maintenance-free technology. The motor/traction package accommodated both regenerative and rheostatic braking facilities.

The new trains were designed to avoid the shortcomings of the 1983 stock and were provided with wide double-doorways (except at car ends) with wide standbacks at one side and a circulating area on the other which could either accommodate wheelchairs or passengers leaning against cushioned perches. The cost of this, of course, was a significant drop in seating capacity to 32 per driving motor and 34 in the other cars – a total of just 200 per train but perhaps rather less unpleasant for those obliged to stand (for whom there is a nominal capacity of 800). Improved service levels would help those travelling farther afield to still get seats.

The first of the new trains was delivered to London Underground on 18th July 1996 and was shown to the press on 9th January 1997 at Stratford where a new track was available for trials. The first train entered passenger service on 24th December 1997 on a Wembley Park to Stanmore shuttle, with trains infiltrated into normal passenger service from 6th January 1998. The conversion of the service to the new trains was achieved quickly, with the last 1983 stock train running on 9th July 1998. Since only about 30 trains were required to support the existing Jubilee Line service, the balance of trains were taken by road to Stratford Market depot for storage and testing.

Two of the 1996 stock Jubilee Line trains on test when new outside Stratford station, just south of Stratford Market Depot. Railtrack's North Woolwich line is seen on the right. LUL

The extended Jubilee Line

From the beginning of the planning process there was a determined effort to avoid repeating the mistakes made when the Victoria Line was built, where stations were virtually built down to a price determined by restrictive government funding – in consequence the line was overwhelmed by traffic in less than 20 years. In seeking to make stations as future-proof as possible, London Underground was in a sense assisted by the new safety regime which encouraged improved space for circulation and required better evacuation facilities, some of which impacted on normal means of access. This time funding was forthcoming and stations with built-in capacity for at least 50 years of optimistic traffic growth were specified.

All stations were to have multiple escalators, sufficient to provide adequate standby when machines were necessarily out of service for maintenance. They were also to have limited lift facilities from street to platform level (not always in one stage) to offer proper access for disabled or encumbered passengers. Platform edge doors were a new feature in London; although specified to help manage airflows they had the obvious secondary benefit of improving safety at the interface between train and platform, a source of some worrying accidents and continuing suicide attempts; they would also reduce platform noise and dust, and help to keep rubbish off the track. The doors are of toughened glass, aligning with those of the trains when fully berthed, and slide behind a toughened glass screen; they can be opened manually for maintenance and in emergencies. Station finishes were to make extensive use of concrete, and lighting was to be concealed where possible, with natural daylight a feature where practicable. A decision was made at an early stage that each of the new stations would be designed independently of the others by different architects.

Green Park station was of course opened as part of Stage I of the Jubilee Line, but the layout was not entirely satisfactory, with interchange with the Piccadilly Line requiring a visit to ticket hall level. Works were therefore undertaken to construct a new interchange subway and staircases between these two lines. At the same time the opportunity was taken to install passenger lifts for the benefit of mobility impaired passengers using the Jubilee Line, and an emergency escape facility within a new ventilation shaft. The extension diverged from the existing line just to the south of Green Park, for which purpose it was necessary to construct 'step plate' junctions. These were cast iron tunnels built around the old tunnels, and whose diameter increased in 'steps' until at the far end the old and new tunnels could be accommodated; when completed, the old tunnel within could be dismantled and the new pointwork installed.

Westminster was probably the most difficult site at which to build a Jubilee Line station, mainly as a result of objections from MPs at the Palace of Westminster to earlier plans to excavate a new ticket hall underneath Parliament Square. In consequence it was necessary to excavate a massive box 75m by 27m, and 32m deep. This required demolition of the existing station building and basement ticket hall, and all surrounding buildings. The District Line platforms crossed the site almost on a diagonal and had at an early stage to be supported on a new bridge 15m below ground level; the need to work around a live railway in the midst of this cavern remained a daunting challenge throughout. To add to the problem the District needed lowering about half a metre to improve headroom for the supports for the new parliamentary building above. The Jubilee Line platforms were built one below the other, and both below the District, an arrangement deemed likely to minimise possible subsidence to the Clock Tower on the other side of Bridge Street, under which the platforms lie. The awkward layout requires 17 escalators and five lifts to service efficiently, but the District Line shares the benefits, having previously only had stairway access. Escape stairs are provided at Storey's Gate and on the Embankment.

At Waterloo it was fortunately possible to combine the Jubilee Line planning work with the need to accommodate the requirements of the new international terminal. The outcome was an additional flight of escalators (parallel to the existing ones serving the Northern and Bakerloo Lines from the main line station), together with a new ticket hall in the Waterloo Road area, and new links from the buses to both the Underground and main line stations. The Jubilee Line platforms serve the lowest level within the station, and have resulted in eight new escalators, two lifts and two travolators (linking the Jubilee with the Northern/Bakerloo part of the station). At the same time existing escalators have been refurbished, which also required temporary closure of the 'Shell' ticket hall.

Southwark station provides a new transport facility south of the river at the junction of Blackfriars Road and The Cut. But the main justification for a station here was the ability to provide a good interchange with the very busy main line platforms at Waterloo East, which would have been difficult to achieve from the enlarged Waterloo Underground complex itself. The Jubilee Line was routed directly beneath the main line viaduct and the link from the lower Jubilee Line concourse was made to the eastern end of the main line platforms.

A good sense of the highly complicated work at Westminster can be gained in this view. The escalators connecting the District and Circle Lines with the Jubilee are on the right.

Facing page **Southwark station and connection to Waterloo East under construction.** LUL

Above **View from the track crossover at North Greenwich, February 1997, prior to laying of the current rails.** LUL

Although the existing ticket hall at London Bridge was opened only in 1967 and served just the Northern Line, it was already quite inadequate for prevailing traffic. Furthermore the Northern Line platforms below were hopelessly congested in the peaks, and traffic was rising. As a result, plans had been formulated to improve facilities at ticket hall level, and to build a new southbound platform, allowing conversion of the existing one into a central concourse to improve distribution of people. Funding shortage delayed the works, but the authorisation of the Jubilee extension allowed them to be picked up as part of the larger programme and planning proceeded accordingly. The outcome was two new ticket halls, one beneath the arches of the main line station and the other serving the community in Borough High Street; the existing Northern Line ticket hall was enlarged. Nineteen new escalators were provided (seven connecting directly to the main line platforms) and two lifts.

Left **Station platforms on the Jubilee line extension have plain finishes in most cases. Attractive seating adds colour at Bermondsey.**
Capital Transport

Below **View from the booking hall at Bermondsey showing the large area of glazing.**
Capital Transport

Bermondsey is another new station designed to improve public transport in an area otherwise not well served by railway. Three escalators and one lift provide access to platform level. Although immediate usage is not thought likely to be more than around 2000 passengers in each peak, the long term impact on the area may well be very significant, with both Canary Wharf and Central London brought within a no-change ten minute trip.

Canada Water station serves a vicinity bordering the Docklands redevelopment area and will greatly assist local regeneration. It also provides an interchange with the East London Line by means of new platforms constructed largely during that line's temporary closure to enable tunnel strengthening works to take place. Eight escalators and three lifts have been provided, serving both lines. The main concourse has a high circular ceiling with glazed walls.

Glass again features heavily at Canada Water in an attempt to maximise daylight at the lower levels of the station. The rotunda is essentially a light well illuminating the escalators from the intermediate concourse down to the Jubilee Line lifts. Capital Transport

Canada Water station, in common with Stratford, Canning Town and North Greenwich, offers convenient interchange facilities with bus services. Capital Transport

Facing page **Canary Wharf station under construction.** LUL

Above **One of the two similar entrances to the station, the other 'mothballed' until the Canary Wharf development is more advanced. Very visible here is the glass roof designed to allow daylight to reach the lower levels of the station.** Capital Transport

Canary Wharf station is, of course, the *raison d'etre* of the Jubilee Line extension, and is appropriately commodious in order to cater for some 16,000 passengers an hour each peak. The station box is 280m by 32m, and 24m deep. The site is mainly constructed within the former West India dock, which needed to be drained prior to work starting. The station has two entrances surrounded by massive glass canopies. Each leads to a substantial intermediate concourse containing ticket facilities and other amenities. Initially only the west end ticket hall has been opened, the east end (also finished) awaiting completion of the later stages of the Canary Wharf development.

The wide Canary Wharf platform features exceptionally large name signs, dwarfing the waiting passengers in this view. Capital Transport

North Greenwich station was principally intended to facilitate the regeneration of the otherwise largely inaccessible North Greenwich peninsula, a significant area of which for over a hundred years having been devoted to gas production and storage. The design proceeded on the basis that it had maximum potential as a major transport interchange, both from buses from the south-east and from cars from the same sector, for which purpose a 1000 space car park was built. Three platform roads were built here, reflecting the future possibility that with traffic to the west somewhat heavier than that to the east some trains might be reversed. It also accommodates the possibility of a future branch to the Royal Docks area. Nine escalators and four lifts have been installed here. Of course, when the station was designed there was no hint that the fervour whipped up by the discovery of an approaching millennium would result in the arrival of a millennium dome right next door; however the logic of building it on vacant land and using the surplus transport potential of a nearby brand new railway linked to central London was inescapable, and so it came to be. It was this high quality transport link with central London, coupled with enormous vacant space adjacent, that in March 1996 resulted in the decision to build the Millennium Dome in Greenwich rather than Birmingham. Fortunately, the line's planned March 1998 opening date gave plenty of leeway for slippage in the run-up to 31st December 1999.

Extensive use of dark blue tiling and glazing is made at North Greenwich station, the first subsurface station on the extension to open, and thereby the first on the system to bring platform doors into passenger service.
Capital Transport

Red brick is extensively used at West Ham from the platforms through to the new booking hall across from the Silverlink and southbound Jubilee tracks. Capital Transport

Inevitably likened to an airport building, the large and airy terminal station at Stratford is now a major interchange between Underground, National Rail and DLR services. Capital Transport

Between Canning Town and Stratford the line shadows the North London Line, which it runs more or less alongside at surface level. At Canning Town itself the island platform is covered by the platforms and tracks of the DLR, whilst at West Ham a new ticket hall has been built and interchange with the District Line and main Southend line. Stratford, the terminus, has gained a three-platform Jubilee Line station, together with profound changes to the existing Central Line and main line station with which it is integrated, and an impressive new bus station.

The Running tunnels on the extension are of 4.35m or 4.4m diameter, somewhat larger than most tube tunnels built hitherto. One reason for this was the desire to incorporate a continuous narrow platform ledge proposed initially to facilitate emergency passenger detrainment but now designated for use only by emergency services; of course the 12ft diameter of the existing line precluded exploiting the space for larger trains. The only other example of this detrainment facility was in the single bore Finchley Road Metropolitan tunnels during the time they were used by compartment stock with no end doors. The larger size also helps reduce the 'piston' effect of trains moving air and creating high winds which raise dust.

The first section of tunnel construction started on 25th May 1994 at Jubilee Gardens near Waterloo with boring west from Canary Wharf following early in September. By November the first of the eight river crossings had been completed, with the first link-up of the separate boring sections achieved in December. On 21st September 1995 the tunnel boring achieved the longest stretch of continuous tunnel thus far, from Green Park to London Bridge, at 4.5km, and the following month one tunnel boring machine broke tunnelling records by hitting 254m in one week near North Greenwich. In March 1995 some 85 per cent of tunnels were complete and on 6th August 1996 the final 'breakthrough' occurred.

Between Canada Water and Canary Wharf the twin tunnels pass through the Thanet sands, and the contractor decided to use a Bentonite shield (developed from the New Cross experiment) to deal with this notoriously difficult ground.

Jubilee Line extension running tunnel showing the emergency walkway on the left and the resilient trackform mounted on concrete sleepers. The conductor rails are of the new, high conductivity aluminium type, topped with a stainless steel running surface. The tunnel construction in unbolted concrete segments is clear, together with the wedge-shaped key pieces used to lock the segments home. LUL

Exterior and interior views of the impressive depot at Stratford. QA Photos

All was not, however, good news. Whilst most of the running tunnel construction was comparatively straightforward a new technique had been used at a number of places, especially at some crossovers, platforms and passageways. Known as the New Austrian Tunnelling Method (NATM), it involved spraying concrete onto a metal substructure designed ultimately to provide reinforcement properties. Although the technique has shown itself to be quite satisfactory, the unfortunate collapse in October 1994 of a non-LT tunnel being constructed at Heathrow using the same method naturally caused some concern within the industry and work using this technique on the JLE had to stop pending investigation; work using NATM resumed in January 1995, having caused some dislocation to the overall project plan.

A new depot was needed to serve the extended Jubilee Line, and the former fruit and vegetable market site at Stratford was chosen. This depot now provides dedicated maintenance facilities for all Jubilee Line trains, although stabling facilities are retained at Stanmore sidings and Neasden Depot. The depot building is regarded as having some architectural significance and is 190m by 110m in size, covering 11 roads. Altogether the depot has a capacity of 33 trains. A new feature is the raising of some tracks on stanchions to facilitate work underneath the trains and the removal of equipment without the necessity for pits. Cars are also lifted by means of jacks rather than the traditional overhead crane.

The Jubilee Line extension project has generated a need for an additional 118 escalators, increasing LUL's total for these machines by nearly 40 per cent. The machines, provided by O&K have a maximum rise not exceeding 20m, avoiding the difficulties inherent in much longer machines. This substantial fleet increase arises from a desire to avoid flights with fewer than three machines in parallel (building in some redundancy), and the double-ending of most stations. The additional machines are required mainly for the numerous new interchanges being built, where, often, more than one flight of escalators is required because of site conditions. All stations have access for mobility impaired passengers using lifts, generally in one or two stages, depending on ticket hall configuration.

The Extension also benefits from much enhanced ventilation systems. In July 1999, with outside temperatures reaching 30°C the tunnels in the North Greenwich area were maintained at a pleasant 16°C. Most tube lines in London are fairly warm, with heat from trains and people being absorbed by the ground surrounding the tunnels and stations and warming the circulating air. On the Jubilee extension powerful fans are installed between as well as at both ends of most stations, helping to keep temperatures down, and in an emergency facilitating the controlled movement of any smoke.

On the subject of smoke, the extension is constructed to exceptional safety standards with all possible care taken to avoid materials which contribute to fire or smoke loading, and with robust fire compartmentation separating passenger areas from equipment. Nevertheless an objective was set that a combined train-load of passengers, and an additional platform load, should in the event of a fire be able to reach a place of safety within 6 minutes (this is usually the lower station concourse which will have access to fresh air drawn in by the fans). However, to comply with a further requirement that an exit will be available within 18m of any dead end, stations all have either one or two escape shafts located away from the normal exits. In addition some of the inter-station ventilation shafts are equipped as emergency escape routes.

Canary Wharf station has a bank of five escalators at each end with further escalators leading from the booking hall to the platforms. Capital Transport

The platform doors are to the same design at each of the new tunnel stations. These ones are at Canada Water. Capital Transport

In order to manage the extended Jubilee Line it was decided to erect a purpose built control centre at Neasden to replace the one at Baker Street which was in adapted accommodation and not conveniently upgradable. The new installation is at the southern end of Neasden Depot and incorporates staff training facilities on site. A proposal to move the Metropolitan and Hammersmith & City Line controls there was abandoned. All communication facilities are also supervised from the new control room, which opened on 26th July 1998 as the first part of a phased process.

It was the intention to install a fully automatic signalling system on the Jubilee Line, coupled with the latest radio-based, moving block automatic train protection technology. Unfortunately considerable difficulties arose in obtaining a satisfactory design, bearing in mind that on the existing railway it needed to be superimposed upon older technology and it would have been the largest system of that type in the world thus far. Notwithstanding the contractual obligations, as construction of the extension progressed it became increasingly obvious that the contractor would not be able to have a fully working and tested system in place by anything like the proposed opening date, and a credible fall-back position was required. In consequence efforts were necessarily switched towards a basic installation of fixed block technology, partly using recovered equipment from the Central Line resignalling. This has the obvious disadvantages of restricting train services initially to 24 trains an hour (sufficient in the short term) and generating fears of likely disruption and inconvenience as the new equipment is installed in due course – precisely the difficulties endured by Central Line passengers for some years.

In the absence of the promised fully automatic signalling system, conventional track circuit signalling was installed with two-aspect signals and air-operated points and trainstops. Interlocking at Green Park, Waterloo, London Bridge, Canary Wharf, North Greenwich, Stratford and Stratford Market Depot was provided by local solid state computerised equipment, supervised from Neasden Control Centre (or the depot control tower in the case of the depot). The electro-mechanical interlockings were retained elsewhere on the older sections of the line as they were not life-expired.

Communications on the extension are to the most modern standards on the Underground. At stations, all standard announcements are digitised, enabling consistent, clear messages to be transmitted quickly. In addition stations are designed to address the usual acoustic shortcomings with special finishes, and announcement volume is adjusted to take into account variations in background noise, such as the arrival of a train. In addition to the dot-matrix indicators on the platforms, which show the destination and waiting times for the next few trains, additional indicators have been provided at ticket hall level to warn of any significant delays or service interruptions but passengers ought to be aware of before starting a journey. For the first time coverage of all public areas has been achieved by closed circuit television, not only aiding station controllers to manage the stations, but with facilities to send images to the line's main control centre at Neasden and the British Transport Police.

From the beginning of the extension's construction the opening date had been planned as 28th March 1998. However, a variety of setbacks during construction meant that this date became increasingly unachievable and in March 1997 a revised opening date in September 1998 was quoted. The main difficulties at that time appeared to be an inability to recover from the delays the NATM construction debacle had introduced, coupled with the absence of a signalling system and significant construction problems in the Westminster area. Despite initial denials, in August 1997 rumours of further delays proved to be true, and LUL announced the opening date was being again shifted back to March 1999.

Nor was this the end. Mounting concern about the difficult works at the Westminster end began to generate options to open the extension in phases, with the link with the existing line opening last. Finally, during spring 1998 and amidst mounting external pressure, the American construction company, Bechtel, was called in to examine the state of play. They concluded that there were some risks that the complete extension would not be ready by 1st January 2000, particularly at the Westminster end where schedules continued to slip; nonetheless the line east of Waterloo was achievable if progress were kept up (though labour troubles with subcontractors did not bode well). A significant problem was achieving final Health & Safety 'sign off' of completed station systems.

As a result of the analysis Bechtel were asked to put in a high level project team to supervise and expedite completion; upon appointment they immediately and confidently announced a phased opening would occur. Stratford–North Greenwich would open in spring 1999, North Greenwich–Waterloo would open in late summer 1999, with the final link to Green Park following in late autumn. Apart from general disappointment from potential users of the line (especially at Canary Wharf, where users of the increasingly hard pressed DLR were noticing train seats being removed to make more space) the government and managers of the Millennium Dome were beginning to panic and demanded fall-back plans – 31st December 1999 was not a date which could be postponed.

A further complication during this process was the proposed initial payment of £95m to London Underground by Canary Wharf Ltd under the private sector funding regime which had spawned the project in the first place, and upon which LUL was relying. Under this regime LUL had to have the line open by a certain date, which it was now going to miss. In the end, protracted negotiations avoided the potential catastrophe of this contribution being lost. A long term view of the value of the Jubilee Line was now being taken, with Phase 2 of the Canary Wharf development (which depended on the line) beginning while the haggling was still going on.

It was not initially intended to include a station at Southwark on the extension, but its potential usefulness to local residents, commercial developments and as a connection to Waterloo East Main Line station led to a decision to add it. The architects here have consciously referred to the classic Holden style of the 1930s for the booking hall, while at the foot of the first bank of escalators triangular sheets of glass and deep blue fabric provide a dramatic view to and from the platform level.
Capital Transport

Phase I between Stratford and North Greenwich opened on Friday 14th May 1999, just a few days short of the 20-year anniversary of Jubilee Line Stage 1. The opening ceremony was presided over by the Deputy Prime Minister (John Prescott) who was keen to emphasise the tremendous benefits the line would bring when completed. Initially trains only ran Mondays to Fridays, and then not into the evening – traffic on the initial section would be light and the capacity at quiet times was better made available for the engineer's trains to and from the uncompleted sections.

The initial timetable operated from 06.22 to 20.07 on weekdays (07.20 to 20.07 Sundays), with a basic 6-minute service requiring just four trains. In fact the timetable was available for trial operations from 1st March 1998, although regular workings of the empty trains for trial purposes did not begin until Thursday 1st April 1999.

Phase 2 opened in two parts – initially from North Greenwich to Bermondsey at 15.30 on the afternoon of 17th September 1999 and thence to Waterloo on 24th September. London Bridge did not open until 7th October and Southwark until November. In the meantime trains non-stopped. Canada Water station had already opened to East London Line passengers on 19th August 1999. However, train services continued to be restricted to Monday to Friday daytime operations so that engineering work could continue in the evenings and at weekends.

Through running in passenger service, seven days a week, began from start of traffic on Saturday 20th November 1999. At this point Charing Cross station ceased to be served by Jubilee Line passenger trains. Early thoughts that it could be used for special workings, or in an emergency, became increasingly impractical as it was realised the escalators were nearly life expired and the cost of replacements could not have been justified. The first train from the original Jubilee Line onto the extension was scheduled to leave West Hampstead at 05.08. Engineering work was taking place north of this station and the first train had been intended to reach it, out of service, from the Stratford end. A signal failure at North Greenwich delayed its journey by almost an hour and so the train thereafter took passengers. At about 06.15 it left West Hampstead, without ceremony, for Stratford. Southwark station opened on the same day, as did the Lewisham extension of the Docklands Light Railway, connecting with the Jubilee Line at Canary Wharf. The final station to open, Westminster, came into service on the afternoon of 22nd December 1999, but it was in an atmosphere more of relief than celebration. The immovable deadline had only just been beaten.

The first scheduled passenger train from the old to the new section of the Jubilee Line left West Hampstead with 20 ordinary passengers and one enthusiast. The trip was made without ceremony of any kind and without any announcement of its significance over the public address. This view shows it en route. The bright interiors of the trains have been well received by passengers. Capital Transport